Hamlyn all-colour paperbacks

Robert Goodden

Butterflies

illustrated by Joyce Bee

Hamlyn - London
Sun Books - Melbourne

FOREWORD

In a small book of this kind it is not possible to cover the thousands of species of butterflies that live in all parts of the world. It is my object to convey an impression of the major families found in the different geographical regions and I have highlighted some of the most interesting individual species. I am indebted to the artist, Joyce Bee, for her superb illustrations and her deep understanding of the subject which has contributed to the quality and accuracy of the paintings.

There is an increasing interest in butterflies which may be partly due to the current and very necessary moves towards world conservation of wildlife. Butterflies are suffering from man's development as much as other wildlife. A greater understanding of Lepidoptera, the life histories and their requirements will go a long way towards helping to prevent the present decline. By breeding and studying butterflies both in captivity and in the wild we can learn how to help them live unmolested in unspoilt localities. It is not always realized that butterflies can be bred at home with simple equipment. I hope that this book will enable anyone, without previous knowledge, to take a keener interest and even start rearing butterflies from which one learns more than any book can convey.

R.C.G.

Published by The Hamlyn Publishing Group Limited
London · New York · Sydney · Toronto
Hamlyn House, Feltham, Middlesex, England
In association with Sun Books Pty Ltd, Melbourne

Copyright © The Hamlyn Publishing Group Limited 1971
Reprinted 1972

ISBN 0 600 00073 7
Phototypeset by Filmtype Services Limited, Scarborough, England
Colour separations by Schwitter Limited, Zurich
Printed in Holland by Senefelder, Purmerend

CONTENTS

4   Introduction
5   Life cycle
24   Butterfly migration
25   Colouring and marking
     of butterflies
36   Nomenclature
37   Breeding butterflies from
     caterpillars
41   Butterfly families of the
     world
62   Butterfly habitats and
     seasons
68   Collecting equipment and
     methods
74   Making a reference
     collection
80   Breeding butterflies
99   Butterflies of the
     different geographical
     regions
99   Europe
108 North America
117 Central and South America
126 Africa and Madagascar
136 Australia, New Guinea and
     New Zealand
144 Asia
153 South-west Asia
156 Books to read
157 Index

INTRODUCTION

Butterflies, together with moths, are the second most numerous group of creatures in the animal kingdom after the huge order of beetles, the Coleoptera. The caterpillars of butterflies are plant-feeders, and a few species are pests. Both caterpillars and adults are important as food for birds and reptiles. As pollinators the adults are useful to plants. Butterflies probably do little good or harm to Man but they are fascinating and beautiful creatures.

In many parts of the world butterflies are becoming scarcer. The change of habitat by taking land for building, ploughing up meadowland and chalk downs, cutting down hedges and mowing verges causes more harm even than insecticides and herbicides, though there is little doubt that the use of chemicals in agriculture has a harmful effect.

Lepidopterists (those who study butterflies and moths) are being encouraged to follow their interests by means other than collecting, such as colour photography, where possible. Over-collecting could be a danger to a small colony of butter-flies. There is usually no harm in taking small numbers and to make a proper study it is often necessary to collect a representative sample.

The egg — various forms

THE LIFE CYCLE

There are four stages in the life cycle of a butterfly – egg, caterpillar, chrysalis or pupa, and adult. The caterpillar eats almost continuously: it can increase its weight by up to 1,000 times. It sheds its skin frequently before pupating to allow for growth.

There is a tremendous loss of individuals at all stages. Many predators take their share of a butterfly's brood. Others are lost through disease or unfavourable conditions. One pair of butterflies should on average produce just two more butterflies. If there were no loss at all, a pair of butterflies could in one season produce a total of 3 million individuals.

The duration of each stage varies with the species, temperature and climate. A tropical species might be in the egg for only three days, a caterpillar for eight days, a pupa for seven days, making a total of eighteen days before emergence. In more temperate countries it would take about eight weeks for a fast growing species. Many species take a full year to complete the life cycle and one stage will hibernate. In hot countries a dormant stage may occur during the hot season (aestivation).

The eggs of butterflies
How they differ

Each species of butterfly is recognizable by its egg. The shape, size, colour and pattern is very varied, and it is usually possible to tell which family it comes from, if not the actual species. The Pieridae (Orange Tip, the whites, etc.) have a long bottle-shaped egg which is usually yellow or orange. The Vanessidi (Red Admiral and peacocks) lay eggs which are almost round, green and ribbed. The Lycaenidae (blues and coppers) have round, rather flat eggs, generally white or greyish, which are pitted, and often with a prominent central black spot, in reality a minute aperture called the micropyle. Hesperiidae (the skipper family) are recognizable by their rather flat, almost rectangular eggs, which are generally a shade of yellow or whitish. The swallowtails (family Papilionidae) lay very round eggs, larger than most other butterflies and generally yellow in colour: the birdwings from New Guinea lay eggs the size of the head on a glass-headed pin.

Eggs are worth looking at under a microscope, and with a binocular instrument they are particularly striking.

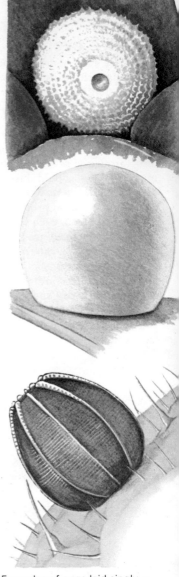

Examples of eggs laid singly — Hairstreak *(top)*, Swallowtail *(middle)*, Comma *(bottom)*

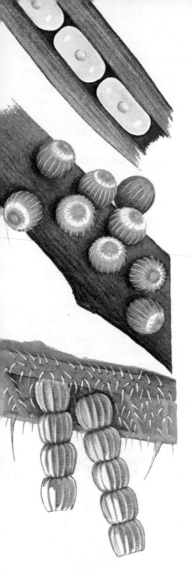

How and where eggs are laid

The female butterfly usually selects the foodplant of the caterpillar on which to lay her eggs and often a particular part of the plant. Orange Tip eggs are found attached to the stem just under the flower-head of garlic mustard and cuckoo flower and they are visible only if you turn the head over. Brimstones select the terminal shoots of buckthorn to lay their eggs on and swallowtails lay on the flower-heads of milk parsley, where the eggs are completely hidden amongst the flowers. The Silver-washed Fritillary does not lay on the caterpillar's foodplant, violet, but in the crevices in the bark of an oak tree near a patch of violets. The larvae hibernate in the bark until they climb down to the ground in the spring.

Often butterflies lay eggs singly or in small groups but many lay in large clusters. Peacocks and Small Tortoiseshells lay clusters on the top shoots of nettle, Large Whites on the underside of cabbage leaves and the European Map Butterfly lays her eggs in long strings hanging beneath a nettle leaf. A few species scatter their eggs on the ground.

Examples of eggs laid in batches — Skipper *(top)*, Japanese Purple Emperor, *Sasakia charonda (middle)*, Map Butterfly *(bottom)*

7

The micropyle and structure

When the egg is first laid it appears to contain nothing but a clear liquid, but an embryo caterpillar gradually develops inside and this living creature needs to be able to breathe. For this purpose there is a minute air hole called the micropyle, situated either at the top or the side of the egg. It is also through this opening that the egg is fertilized in the female's abdomen as it is laid. The egg is passed through the oviduct from the ovary to the egg-laying tube or ovipositor and it is only at this stage that, if the female has mated, the egg becomes fertilized.

The outer shell of the egg is made of a substance known as chitin, which is closely allied to the material that the human fingernail is made of. In most butterflies the eggshell is transparent and it is possible to watch the development inside if the egg is fertile. A Swallowtail egg will become slightly orange, then change to grey and finally black as the caterpillar becomes fully formed inside. The caterpillar eats a small hole in the shell and crawls out. Then it settles down to eat part or all of the shell before starting to feed on the foodplant. This seems to be a necessary part of its diet and evidently contains certain vital foods because the caterpillar may die if prevented from eating the shell.

Egg showing micropyle

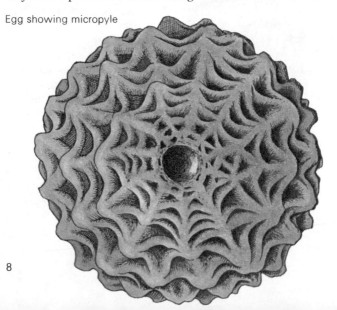

Caterpillars
How they differ

Most butterfly larvae are not hairy though some of the tropical species have coloured tufts. If you find a 'woolly bear' you can be sure that it is the caterpillar of a moth. Caterpillars very often match their backgrounds, so they are very well camouflaged. The Satyridae (the browns) are grass feeders. Their caterpillars are long and pointed at each end with stripes in various shades of green, blending beautifully with their grassy foodplants. Some of the Danaidae (the distasteful milkweed family) have prominent markings in yellow and black which do not camouflage the caterpillar but advertise that it is nasty to eat. The Vanessidi (peacocks and tortoiseshells) often live in tight colonies. They are black with spikes; some of the fritillaries are spiked too. The Small Copper caterpillar is oval and flat so that it seems to be just a small green lump on the leaf. It eats away the cuticle of the leaf and hides in the dip it has made. The Orange Tip caterpillar is green and slender. It is countershaded so that it looks like the seed pods amongst which it feeds.

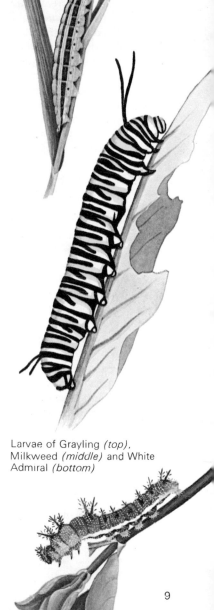

Larvae of Grayling *(top)*, Milkweed *(middle)* and White Admiral *(bottom)*

9

Some of the hairstreaks are difficult to find because, like the Small Copper, they are rather flat and oval and they lie tight against the under-surface of the leaf. The caterpillar of the Comma is slightly spiny and black, but part of the body is striped with brown and the rest white. This, together with its peculiar, curled, resting position on the upper surface of a leaf, makes it look like a bird dropping. The young European Swallowtail larva is black with a white 'saddle' giving a similar effect, but in the third *instar* (that is, stage between moults) this colouring changes to bright green with warning colours in black and orange. Some tropical swallowtails develop remarkable face-like markings with staring eyespots. The Large Skipper Butterfly caterpillar hides itself in a tent of grass held together with silk. In order not to draw attention to itself it is able to catapult its droppings several inches away! It is the droppings, or frass, left by a caterpillar which often leads to its discovery. The Glanville and Heath Fritillary caterpillars feed on plantain; they are small and black with brown and grey spikes all over,

Caterpillars of Brown Hairstreak *(top),* Swallowtail *(middle)* and Large Skipper *(bottom)*

making them look very much like the heads of plantain.

One of the most remarkable of all caterpillars is that of the Large Blue Butterfly (*Maculinea arion*). The life history of this butterfly was unknown until 1915 when Captain Purefoy discovered its fascinating secret. It was known that the eggs were laid on wild thyme flowers but each caterpillar always wandered off the plant and stopped feeding. By careful observation it was eventually discovered that the caterpillar is taken off by an ant to its nest and there fed on ant larvae until it pupates!

Where caterpillars are found

Caterpillars are nearly always on their foodplant, camouflaged beneath the leaves, on the stems or hiding at the foot of the plant. Those which live in colonies seldom hide and are easily seen. There is no particular type of locality where caterpillars live and it is the distribution of the foodplant which determines the range of the caterpillar.

Newly emerged larva eating its egg shell

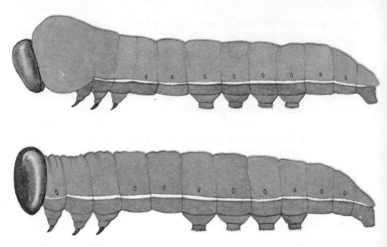

Before *(upper)* and after *(lower)* ecdysis

Skin changing

In order that the caterpillar may grow it has to shed its skin several times during its life. This usually happens four or five times but some species shed their skin more than this. The process of skin changing is called *ecdysis*. The caterpillar spins a silken web on a leaf or stem and takes up a firm position on this web for twenty-four hours or so before the skin actually splits behind the head. Muscular movement forces the skin towards the tail until the skin is completely cast off. Often the new skin is a completely different colour. You can recognize a caterpillar that is about to change by the way it sits humped up and especially by the way the old and empty head capsule protrudes prominently from the new and larger head which is forming under the skin of the first segment. Sometimes this empty head capsule remains on the head of the caterpillar after the rest of the old skin has been shed and has to be deliberately knocked off by the caterpillar. When a caterpillar has just moulted it cannot feed for several hours until the new skin and mouth have hardened. The change to the chrysalis is made in exactly the same way: the skin of the last instar is cast off exposing the as yet unhardened pupal skin.

How caterpillars breathe

In common with all insects, a caterpillar has a series of breathing holes along the sides of its body. There is a pair of these *spiracles* on each segment. Sometimes the spiracles are prominently coloured, sometimes they blend with the overall pattern. When a caterpillar sheds its skin fine, white threads of cuticle are drawn out of the spiracular openings along with the cast off skin. The threads are the linings of the *tracheae* or breathing tubes, a system of branching vessels which supplies oxygen to and removes carbon dioxide from the cells and tissues of the body. There are no lungs and the blood plays little part in the exchange of gases.

The tracheae branch ever more finely into *tracheoles,* which at their termination in or on the surface of the cells they supply are as little as 1/1,000 mm in diameter. The cuticular lining is greatly thinned to allow free movement of molecules of oxygen and carbon dioxide across the walls in contact with the tissues. Exchange is by diffusion alone from the air, along the tracheae and tracheoles, and into the cells. In caterpillars there are no active movements to aid this process. Water may be lost through the spiracles since the air in the tracheae is in contact with the water of the body's cells. Opening and closure of the spiracles is governed by special muscles which serve to regulate the exchange of gases on the one hand and the loss of water on the other. A caterpillar can have its head in water without drowning and even be three quarters immersed without suffering. A larva which has been totally immersed and presumed dead for hours can sometimes be revived by rolling on absorbent paper which withdraws the water from the tracheae.

Respiratory system of an insect

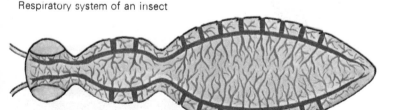

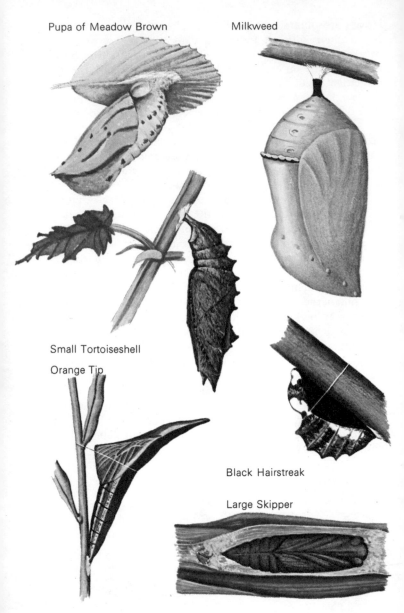

Pupa of Meadow Brown

Milkweed

Small Tortoiseshell

Orange Tip

Black Hairstreak

Large Skipper

14

The importance of silk to caterpillars

Silk is generally associated with silkworms and the spinning of cocoons. Butterfly caterpillars do not spin cocoons but they still need to produce silk. In order to change skin the caterpillar makes a pad of silk onto which it can grip firmly for several days. Some larvae use silk as a lifeline if they lose their grip of a stem; they can crawl up the thread again to their original perch. Silk is also vital for the attachment of the pupa or chrysalis. Some spin a pad, as they do when they are about to change their skin, and hang themselves by the tail. Others again spin a pad to attach the tail to a twig but, with their head upwards, they use silk to spin a girdle to support the head end, right round the body. Solitary caterpillars like the Red Admiral use silk to draw a leaf together, forming a shelter. Some gregarious species spin large and complicated webs on which they live for most of their lives.

The silk is secreted from a silk gland situated in one of the first three segments. It is secreted as a liquid but, in contact with the air, the liquid silk solidifies and becomes a thread. The silk is drawn out by the spinnerets which are usually in the second segment situated immediately beneath and behind the head.

The chrysalides
How they differ

As with the caterpillars camouflage is often necessary to protect the pupae. Some are very well protected indeed. The Black Hairstreak, for example, has a little rounded black pupa with white areas and, like certain caterpillars, often passes as an uninteresting bird dropping. The Orange Tip pupa, though not always formed on the seed head of its foodplant, looks just like a seed pod and changes from green to brown in the autumn like the seed pod. Swallowtails often pupate on reeds and water plants. They can be green or brown, though curiously the colour does not necessarily coincide with that of the background: a mystery that nobody has yet been able to solve!

The chrysalides of the family Nymphalidae hang from their tail end, sometimes from the leaves of their foodplant but more often they can be found hiding some way away. The fritillaries of the genus *Melitaea* are whitish, speckled with black and orange or · with some pattern which disrupts the appearance of their shape. The Vanessidi and the larger fritillaries (*Argynnis*) are usually shades of brown and green to match the foliage and often have either a gold hue or gold and silver spangles which reflect light like a dew drop. Some of the danaids too, have these metallic marks, sometimes just a spot or two, but the tropical euploeas (crow butterflies) often have completely reflective surfaces as shining as mirrors. They look quite unreal and are difficult to see because they reflect their background and appear almost transparent. Pupae of the Satyridae, the large family of browns, are sometimes a translucent green. They may hang in a fairly exposed position amongst grass, but others in this family pupate on the ground, forming a loose silken network with leaves over them, almost like a cocoon. Similarly the skippers usually hide themselves, but in rolled up tubes of grass.

The change from larva to pupa in the Swallowtail Butterfly *(Papilio machaon)*. The larva attaches its tail to a pad of silk and spins a girdle round its thorax. After the skin splits the larva sheds it from the tail end, revealing the pupal skin which hardens into a different shape, recognisable as the chrysalis.

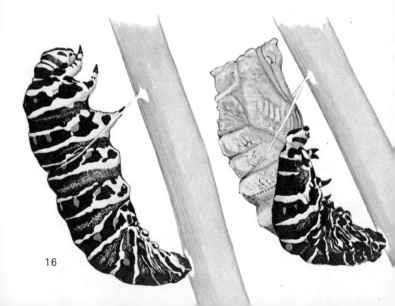

How and where chrysalides are formed

The transformation from the caterpillar to the chrysalis, a lively, hungry and active creature to a static and dormant being which cannot eat, seems almost as much a miracle as the birth of the adult butterfly itself. It is indeed an amazing change and one that is brought about by a particular progression of events. When the caterpillar sheds its skin there is another larger skin beneath the old one. The final change to the pupa is really very similar to the previous moults but the skin beneath is in the shape of the pupa. It is very soft indeed and only takes the proper shape and colour of the pupa after hours of hardening. It is fascinating to watch this change, especially with the pupae which suspend themselves by the tail. The skin splits on the thorax and is gradually worked upwards to the tail end. Then, with a lightning twitch, the tail releases its grip of the silk pad, flicks away the skin and in a split second re-attaches itself before it falls to the ground!

Chrysalides often have to withstand the whole winter in quite exposed situations. They have to be well attached, well camouflaged and able to withstand extremes of weather and temperature.

They survive buried in snow and can endure temperatures

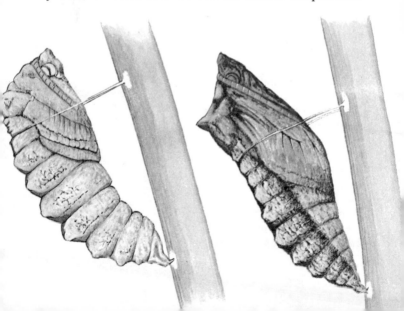

as low as $-24°C$ $(-12°F)$. Even tropical species seem to be able to stand such cold.

There are three ways in which butterflies pupate. Species such as the Nymphalidae hang from tail hooks (known as the cremaster) suspended from a pad of silk. This method is known as *suspensi*. Swallowtails, Lycaenids and pierids attach themselves with a girdle as well as by the cremaster and this method is known as *succincti*. The method of the skippers and browns which lie on the ground or in a shelter is known as *involuti*.

Sexing chrysalides

It is very difficult indeed to sex the pupae of butterflies. An illustration has been chosen which shows the differences in a species of *Papilio,* from Japan. However the appearance of all pupae and their genital markings varies so much that there can be no definite rules laid down. In the male there is generally a small protuberance on the fifth segment from the wing cases towards the tail, but in the female this mark is on the fourth segment. On moth pupae the protuberance is clear, but a strong lens is needed to see it on a butterfly.

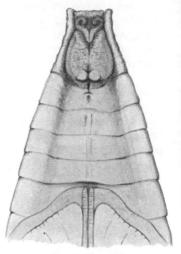

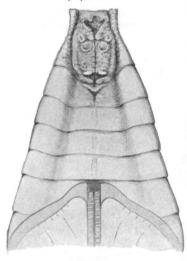

Sexual difference between male *(above)* and female *(below)* Swallowtail pupae

Development of the adult within the chrysalis

When the caterpillar sheds its final skin and becomes a pupa a considerable physical change takes place inside to enable the adult butterfly to form from the caterpillar. The digestive system, nerve ganglia and other vital organs are only slightly altered, but the rest breaks down to a fluid in which the new parts form. The caterpillar is sexually immature but in its later stages the sexual parts are just present. These develop considerably in the pupa. The other parts of the adult butterfly develop from small groups of cells – known as imaginal buds. These cells start to divide and by this means small groups of cells accumulate and gradually assume the adult characteristics. The shape of the pupa is already designed for these changes with covers clearly mapped out for the wingcases, legs, the proboscis, antennae and eyes. In the later stages of development hairs are formed on the head, thorax, abdomen, legs and wings. Then the wing scales form, as yet without any coloration. Finally the wing cases are flooded with the pigment which will eventually colour the scales and give the butterfly its pattern and colouring. It is at this stage that you can see the colour showing through the transparent wing cases. The butterfly dries out a little inside the pupal case and then the case splits on the thorax and the adult butterfly crawls out. Its wings are only a fraction of their eventual size, so it needs to find a suitable place where it can hang to expand its wings and dry out completely.

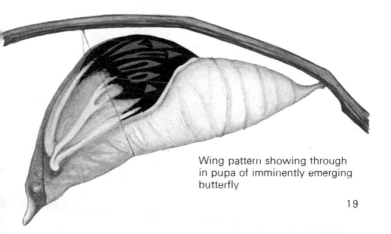

Wing pattern showing through in pupa of imminently emerging butterfly

19

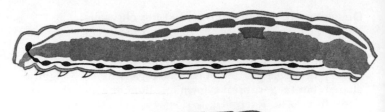

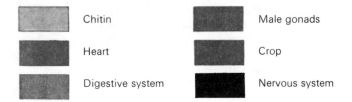

Chitin		Male gonads
Heart		Crop
Digestive system		Nervous system

The internal structure at different stages in the life cycle – larva *(top)*, pupa *(middle)*, adult *(bottom)*

The adult butterfly
Comparison internally with the earlier stages

There are no veins, arteries or capillaries in the circulatory system of an insect. The blood is restricted only by the limits of the insect's body cavity, the *haemocoel*, in which lie the various organs of the body. The tissues are thus bathed in blood rather than supplied by a system of vessels. This is why an insect, particularly a caterpillar, generally dies if the body is punctured – it simply bleeds to death. The blood does not carry oxygen and it contains no corpuscles. It is pumped round the body by the heart, a long, many chambered tube situated dorsally (along the back). Blood enters at the hind end and at the sides (backflow is prevented by valves) and is pumped out at the head end.

The nervous system consists of a chain of nerve centres, known as *ganglia,* connected by a ventral nerve cord which leads from the head along the underside to the tail. The 'brain' is a simple fusion of the ganglia corresponding to the head segments and does not exert the same degree of control over the creature that the brain of a mammal does. The thoracic and abdominal ganglia are of considerable importance in integrating the activity of their appropriate segments. A male praying mantis, for example, is still able to copulate even though the female devours his head during mating.

Food passes from the mouth into the crop where it is digested by enzymes produced in the stomach. The food then passes to the gizzard where it is further ground up and strained so that only fluid matter goes into the stomach. Digested food in the stomach is taken into the body and excretory products are passed on to the hind intestine and thence out of the body. Between the stomach and the hind intestine are very fine tubes known as Malpighian tubes which act as a kidney and separate waste substances from the blood.

The illustrations show the comparison of all these systems in the body of the caterpillar, the chrysalis and the adult. The most striking difference is in the degeneration of the digestive system, which becomes increasingly less important after the caterpillar stage. The nervous system develops and enlarges in the head and thorax.

The 'brain' is quite a lot larger in the adults. The heart is much the same size in all stages. The sexual organs develop mainly in the pupal stage, making their first appearance when the larva is fully grown and about to pupate. These are most noticeable in the female, because of the bulk of the ovaries. In fact the most remarkable thing is the similarity internally between the three stages which are, externally, so completely different in appearance and function.

Expansion of wings

When a butterfly first emerges from the chrysalis, it releases a deposit of pinkish fluid, meconium, which is excretory material built up in the pupal stage. Still with tiny wings it searches for a twig or similar support which it can climb, so as to hang in a position where its wings, when fully expanded, will be clear of other objects which might damage them. It hangs almost motionless, taking in a considerable amount of air through its proboscis and the spiracles. A pressure of air is built up inside the thorax and abdomen and by muscular contraction blood is forced into the short and undeveloped wings. The wings gradually expand and the membranes of the upper and lower surfaces are brought closer together until they almost join by which time the wings have reached their full size. Still the butterfly is not ready to fly; it holds its wings slightly apart, hanging limply. The expansion can be watched in the space of about twenty minutes; the growth can almost be seen. But the butterfly needs at least another hour to dry properly before it can take off and fly in search of nectar.

The wings – comparison of shape

Through the process of evolution in Lepidoptera the hind wings have tended to become smaller in relation to the fore wings and this is shown especially in the hawk moths and skipper butterflies. For efficient flight the two wings on each side have to be securely linked. In moths there is a bristle and catch mechanism to achieve this but, with the exception of an archaic skipper in Australia, this is not found in butterflies. The latter rely on a protruding lobe on the fore-edge of the hind wing that is overlapped by the fore wing and gripped in flight. The butterflies with smaller wings in relation to their body weight have a much faster wing beat. The flight of the small-winged skippers, therefore, much more resembles the frenzied wing beat of a moth. The butterflies with a very large wing area, such as the Asian *Hestia*, glide with a slow and graceful flap of the wing. The Painted Lady flies at an approximate speed of 15 miles per hour (24 kilometres per hour), the Large White at only around 6 m.p.h. (10 km.p.h) (though it can double this if frightened) compared with the faster hawk moths which are capable of about 35 m.p.h. (55 km.p.h). The average wing beat of a butterfly is around 8 to 12 beats per second.

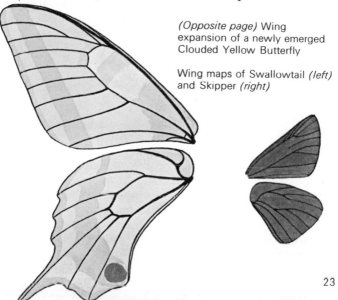

(Opposite page) Wing expansion of a newly emerged Clouded Yellow Butterfly

Wing maps of Swallowtail *(left)* and Skipper *(right)*

23

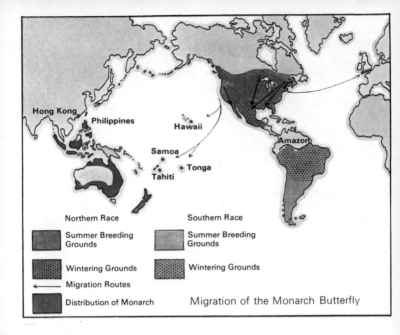

Northern Race

Summer Breeding Grounds

Wintering Grounds

Migration Routes

Distribution of Monarch

Southern Race

Summer Breeding Grounds

Wintering Grounds

Migration of the Monarch Butterfly

BUTTERFLY MIGRATION

It has long been established that the Painted Lady is capable of long migratory flights. It can fly from New Zealand to Australia, right across America and Africa, and from North Africa up to Scandinavia. Migratory flights bring the Painted Lady, Red Admiral, Clouded Yellow and even the Large Cabbage White, which sometimes arrive in spectacular swarms, across the English Channel to the British Isles.

No one has really found the reason for this urge to migrate. It has been observed that a butterfly will try to fly through an obstacle and eventually fly over it rather than deviate a few yards off its course. It is more difficult to record butterfly migrations than those of birds because of their short life-span and the hazards which they encounter. On return flights it is the next generation which travels so one can only hope to record by observation. The Milkweed Butterfly not only migrates long distances across North America in the spring and autumn but has also been recorded crossing the Atlantic. In 1968 over fifty Milkweeds were found in south-west England.

COLOURING AND MARKING OF BUTTERFLIES

The patterns and markings on the wings of butterflies are made up of a mass of tiny coloured scales which overlap each other almost like the tiles on a roof. The colouring in the scales is caused either by a pigment contained in the scales themselves or by the structural character of the scale which refracts light to give off an iridescent colour, though it contains no pigment.

Pigmental colours are either formed from a chemical substance within the insect itself or they can be derived from the foodplant of the caterpillar. The yellow colouring of the Pieridae is given by substances known as *pterines* which are derived from uric acid, and excretory product. The red and orange pigments in the Vanessidi are not related to uric acid and almost certainly come from the larval foodplants. The pigments are interesting to study and in some cases can be extracted or changed experimentally. The red pigments just referred to are affected by oxygen and gradually fade when exposed to the air. A freshly emerged Painted Lady is much brighter than one a week or so old. But if a faded specimen is exposed to chlorine the colour is restored or made even brighter than the original. *Flavones*

Scales on wing of *Parnassius apollo*

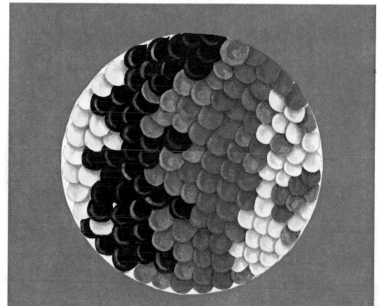

are another group of pigments. In butterflies they have come from the foodplant; they are the pigments which are responsible for the colours ranging from ivory to yellow in flowers. Flavones are found in the Small Heath, Grizzled Skipper and others including the Marbled White. The latter shows a remarkable colour change when exposed to ammonia; the white changes to deep yellow. This ammonia test does not work with the Large White as flavones are not present, but pterines instead. Blacks are derived from *melanin,* the substance which produces freckles in human beings and the black pigment in piebald animals. Green pigments are very rare in butterflies; there are none in British species. Most greens are iridescent structural colours or, in the case of the Bath White and Orange Tip, an optical illusion caused by the intermingling of black and yellow scales.

The iridescent structural colours are caused by light passing through scales made from slightly separated layers or bouncing off scales which are ribbed. The principle is similar to the refraction of light from a soap bubble. All blue colours in Lepidoptera are caused by this means.

Individual wing scales

Protective coloration and mimicry

The coloration and patterning on butterflies contribute greatly to their survival and in some cases are vital. The intricate devices used to camouflage Lepidoptera in all stages are truly remarkable and the species which comes immediately to mind is the Asian Leaf Butterfly. The wings are the exact shape of leaves and the marks on the underside closely resemble ribs and veins. No two individuals are exactly the same shade of colour. Some are marked with spots like leaf decay. The butterfly alights with head downwards and its tail touches its perch and appears to be growing out of it. There are other leaf-like butterflies in the tropics and even species with transparent wings which 'melt' into their backgrounds.

Butterflies which are poisonous or distasteful to birds, far from camouflaging themselves, very often advertise themselves with characteristic or very bright colours which birds learn to avoid. Such colours are known as 'warning colours'.

There are some species which have dull or camouflaged undersides, which conceal them quite well, but they have an additional protection against predators which do manage to find them.

Araschnia levana (Europe)
Spring

Cyaniris argiolus (Europe)
Spring

Precis octavia (Africa)
Dry Season

If surprised, the butterfly suddenly opens its wings to display a flash of bright colouring which startles the predator and gives the butterfly just enough time to escape. This phenomenon is found in many species and is known as 'flash colouring'. The Peacock butterfly combines this flash colouring with the frightening effect of eye-spots that appear and disappear as it opens and closes its wings.

The distasteful butterflies often have very bright and distinctive warning coloration. They can be very poisonous to birds, which quickly learn to recognize and avoid them. Many examples are found in the family Danaidae (the milkweeds and crows). They are common in the tropical and sub-tropical regions. But a number of the Papilionidae (the swallowtails) feed on plants such as Aristolochia that contain toxins; they also benefit from taking on the nauseous flavour. The interesting thing is, that in areas where these butterflies fly, there are invariably other species in different families flying in the same areas with almost identical coloration and marking. Consequently these other butterflies are also avoided by predators which assume them to be the distasteful species. One wonders how this has come about; has it evolved? Has it been brought about by natural selection? No-one can be sure, but in some species the mimetic resemblance to another is so strong that one cannot help feeling that it has not just happened by chance. Females of *Hypolimnas misippus* (Nymphalidae) bear a remarkable resemblance to *Limnas chrysippus* (Danaidae) in both Asia and Africa. In one part of Africa, however, *chrysippus* appears in a different form without a white bar on each fore wing; the female of *misippus* also has a form which has no white bar on the fore wing and exactly resembles this particular geographical form. *Papilio dardanus* in Africa is another species which is polymorphic in the female. It imitates at least half a dozen of the different Danaidae which fly in the same locality. If the species which mimics is more prolific than the model it may sometimes mimic two different species. This prevents birds from finding that the mimic is not in fact distasteful and enables the deception to continue.

Araschnia levana
Summer

Cyaniris argiolus
Summer

Precis octavia
Wet Season

Models (distasteful)

Mimics

Danaus plexippus

Limenitis archippus

Amauris niavius

Papilio dardanus

Euploea mulciber

Papilio paradoxa

Natural variation in butterflies

The pattern on butterflies varies very little and collectors who find a specimen with a minor variation in the marking or colour consider this to be a great asset in their collection. However, there are often variations between specimens from different regions and these are sometimes so marked that the geographical forms are given names. An Australian satyrid looks so different in three different parts of Tasmania, only 100 or so miles apart, that it was considered until recently to be three different species. *Papilio machaon* in Britain not only looks rather different from the Continental race but its habitats are totally different, one living in fens and the other in high mountains, feeding on different plants. Variation is not only geographical but also seasonal with some species. A striking example is the European nymphalid *Araschnia levana,* which in the spring emerges looking like a fritillary, orange-brown and speckled with black; but in the July second brood it appears like a miniature White Admiral, being black with a broad white band across the wings. Another fascinating example is from Africa where *Precis octavia* (Nymphalidae) produces in the wet season a form which is a delightful salmon pink but which in the dry season emerges as a dark blue butterfly with prominent black and red spots. Only by breeding experiments were these forms found to be the same species. In Africa species of *Colotis* (Pieridae) are marked with a great deal of black in the wet season but not so much in the dry season. Such seasonal variation is also seen in the European Large White butterfly, the Holly Blue, and other species, though not to such an extent as in some of the tropical species.

Natural freaks or aberrations do occur in the wild. These are sometimes caused by environmental conditions such as damage by weather to a pupa at the moment when the pigment is forming, or by genetic mutation. On very rare occasions halved gynandromorphs are found in which the insect is half male and half female. This is very spectacular in a species such as the Chalk Hill Blue where the male is blue and the female brown. Temperature affects the formation of the pupa: some breeders deliberately produce artificial varieties by using extremes of temperature.

Abdomens of male *(left)* and female *(right)* Swallowtail

Distinguishing the sexes

With some butterflies it is not very easy to distinguish between the male and the female but by careful examination of the abdomen and genitalia it is possible to see a difference. The abdomen of the female is generally fatter and at the tail more rounded than the male, which has a much more pointed tip. The male has claspers, triangular plates, with which he grips the female when mating. These are prominent in some of the swallowtails. Females sometimes have more rounded wings but this difference is usually very subtle. Some male skippers, fritillaries and euploeas have dark patches of scent scales, as a rule on the forewing; females do not have these markings. These scales, known as *androconia,* give off a faint perfume to attract the female in courtship. A great many species of butterflies are in fact sexually dimorphic, the Brimstone, for example, has a bright yellow male and a whitish female. The blues (Lycaenidae) have blue males while the females are brown. As there are many of these 'easy' species, it is not difficult with a little experience to learn to distinguish those with less marked differences.

Wing patterns of male *(left)* and female *(right)* Clouded Yellows

The differences between butterflies and moths

It is very difficult to draw a strict biological line to separate butterflies from moths; indeed in some countries the difference is hardly recognized. In trying to draw up characteristic differences exceptions are nearly always found. Certainly moths usually fly at night, but a great many are day fliers and just as bright as butterflies to look at. Moths tend to have fatter and furrier bodies, but some butterflies have fat furry bodies too. Moths often rest with their wings folded over their bodies, but so do some butterflies; furthermore many moths rest with their wings spread out like a butterfly. There are, however, some characteristics which are less confusing. The bristle and catch mechanism (*frenulum* and *retinaculum*) used to join the fore wings and hind wings in moths is not found in butterflies (with one exception). But the best distinguishing features are the antennae which, in butterflies, always have a thickened, clubbed end. Moths do not have this; the ends are either feathery, pointed or blunted at the end, but not clubbed.

The antennae of butterflies *(right)* compared with those of moths *(left)* Moth antennae are never headed or clubbed.

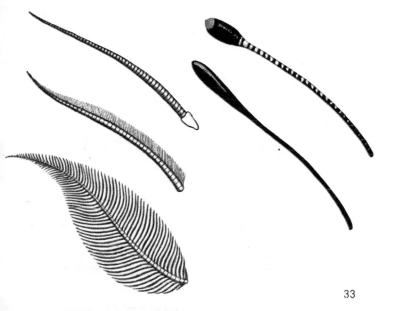

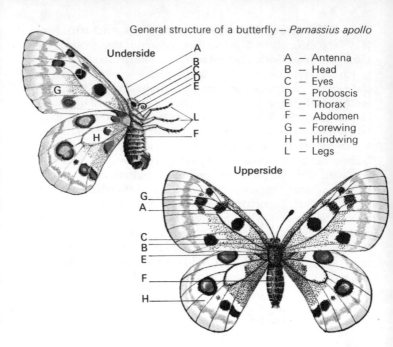

General structure of a butterfly – *Parnassius apollo*

Underside

A
B
C
D
E
L
F
G
H

Upperside

G
A
C
B
E
F
H

A — Antenna
B — Head
C — Eyes
D — Proboscis
E — Thorax
F — Abdomen
G — Forewing
H — Hindwing
L — Legs

The external structure of the adult butterfly

The body of an insect is very different from that of a bird or mammal; it has no bones or internal skeleton. Insects have an outer shell or casing made of chitin. This *exoskeleton* is composed of a number of segments of chitin (*skelerites*) joined together with soft membranes.

There are three principal divisions to an insect's body, the head, thorax and abdomen. The head bears the compound eyes, antennae and mouthparts; on the thorax are the three pairs of legs and the two pairs of wings. The abdomen has no appendages. The wings are attached to strong muscles on either side of the thorax. They consist of two thin transparent membranes, between which run the veins. The wing shape and venation are important features in the classification of butterflies and the venation, in particular, often character-izes a family. The six legs are multi-jointed and they too play a part in classification. At the end of the foot, the *tarsus*, there is a two-pronged claw which enables the butterfly to grip firmly when at rest. There is usually a soft pad also, and curiously it is through this that the butterfly tastes!

The head of a butterfly is largely taken up by the compound eyes which are situated on either side of it. The compound eye is quite unlike our own, being made up of thousands of facets. It is very sensitive to light, though it probably does not have very accurate vision. Being sensitive to light the eye also records movement, warning the butterfly of danger, and a very wide angle of vision is covered. In addition to the compound eyes there are usually about three minute single eyes (*ocelli*) situated on the forehead. From between the eyes, the antennae project, with sense organs leading to the brain. The antennae are sensitive to touch particularly and to smell. It is also possible that they are able to receive radio waves given off by other individuals, but this still has to be properly investigated. The proboscis is a curled tube, like a watch spring, which the insect uncurls and uses to probe flowers for nectar. It is in fact two semi-circular appendages which it joins together to form a tube. In the walls of the proboscis are strong muscles, nerves and tracheae. A butterfly can only take liquid food and has no chewing mouthparts.

Head of a butterfly — Glanville Fritillary

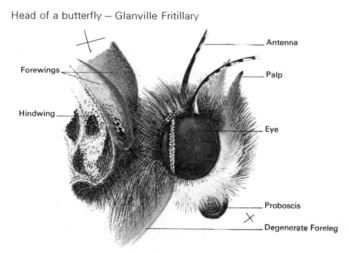

Forewings

Hindwing

Antenna

Palp

Eye

Proboscis

Degenerate Foreleg

NOMENCLATURE

The system of naming butterflies

The table below shows the line of classification of the English Swallowtail, *Papilio machaon*, subspecies *britannicus*. The binominal system of naming was introduced by Linnaeus in the 18th century and Latin or Greek words usually provide the names. If a species is named after a person it is expressed in a latinized form. These names are international and used by zoologists throughout the world, regardless of their own language. This international system, therefore, has great advantages over the use of common names in different tongues. The first name (always spelt with a capital letter) is the generic name. A genus is a group of closely allied species. The second name (written in small letters) is the name of the species of butterfly. If there is a subspecies, its name is written third as in the example below, but many species have no further sub-division. The different species are classified by characteristics such as the genitalia, wing venation, antennae, shape of wing, etc. and the genera accordingly are ranged in families.

Phylum	Arthropoda	Insects, centipedes, crustaceans, spiders
Class	Insecta	Insects
Sub-class	Pterygota	Winged insects and those wingless forms which have evolved from winged insects
Division	Endopterygota	Insects whose wings develop inside the body
Order	Lepidoptera	Butterflies and moths
Sub-order	Heteroneura	Species whose wing venation is different in the fore and hind wings
Super-family	Papilionina	All the butterflies
Family	Papilionidae	Swallowtails, birdwings, apollos etc.
Genus	*Papilio*	Swallowtails
Species	*machaon*	One kind of swallowtail
Sub-species	*britannicus*	Race of *Papilio machaon* found in Britain

BREEDING BUTTERFLIES FROM CATERPILLARS

The chapters up to this point have outlined the basic principles that one needs to know about the life history and structure of butterflies. The practical aspect of rearing butterflies is considerably more interesting and can be very easy if the right species is chosen. Breeding butterflies in general is dealt with in a later chapter but here the intention is to show how simple it is to rear some butterflies of an 'easy' species from the caterpillar stage, without starting on any ambitious projects or using any complicated equipment. As an example the Small Tortoiseshell (*Aglais urticae*) has been chosen. This is a European vanessid butterfly from the family Nymphalidae. It is multi-brooded and feeds on nettles. Counterparts of this species may be found in most parts of the world.

Tortoiseshell larvae are found in June and July and the habitat they like is a patch of nettles isolated in a field, or at the edge. Sometimes they are found on nettle patches in gardens and even in derelict building sites. The larvae cluster and can be spotted by their web.

Small Tortoiseshell laying eggs on a nettle leaf

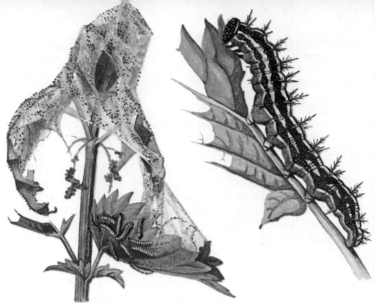

Young larvae of Small Tortoiseshell on a web *(left)*
Fully grown caterpillar of Small Tortoiseshell *(right)*

Shake only a dozen of the whole cluster off into a bag:
an ordinary paper bag is ideal. Put some nettle in so they
can feed and tightly screw up the neck of the bag so they cannot
escape. If you take too many larvae you will not be able to
look after them properly and it is very important that some
should be left to continue in the wild state.

If the caterpillars are still very small and tightly clustered
they will probably escape from a cage so they must be in a
container which will prevent this. The simplest method is to
use a transparent plastic sandwich box, roughly 17 × 12 × 5
cm (7 × 5 × 2 in). Line the bottom with paper (slightly
absorbent if possible), put in a sprig of nettle and then the
larvae. The box does not need air holes; caterpillars breathe
very little and there is plenty of air trapped inside the box.
It is important to keep the lid tight so that the foodplant remains
fresh – wilted food is bad for larvae.

The box needs cleaning out *every* day and fresh food
supplies are needed daily. Take out the lining with the old

food and the larvae, replace it with a new liner and fresh food and then put back the larvae as gently as possible. As they curl up you will find a spoon useful to pick them up in. The larvae grow quite quickly and should, as soon as they are big enough, be put into a larger cage.

If you have not got a cage you can improvise very easily. A large confectionery box or grocer's carton can be converted by cutting out panels from the top, front and sides (back also if you like) and covering these with muslin or netting, as used in dressmaking. Make sure the edges are firmly glued down, because caterpillars escape easily. If the box does not have a lid, the entrance can be at the top, by means of a piece of netting laid over the box and tied round with string. When the cage is ready, cut a good bunch of nettle and stand the bunch in a jar of water to keep the leaves fresh. Put paper in the bottom, stand the nettle in the box and against one of the walls. Put the larvae in, all on the foodplant if possible, but if any are on the floor they will climb up, as long as the plant is touching one wall of the cage.

Another method is to make a bag of netting about 30 to 45 cm (12 × 18 in) and open at both ends. This can be slipped

Improvised cage for larvae

over the bunch of nettles, tied at the bottom, and the larvae put in from the top. Tie the top firmly and the caterpillars will feed quite happily inside. Nettle stood in water needs to be changed about once every two days, or sooner if it starts to wilt. Do not give larvae wet food.

When the larvae come to pupate, they will hang up either on the foodplant or at the top of the cage. They must not be pulled off or disturbed too much. The change to the chrysalis will take three or four days. The chrysalides are best left in position so that the butterflies hatch two to three weeks later, in the most natural conditions possible. If it is hot and dry the pupae should be gently sprayed occasionally (in the natural state they have dew each night).

Breeding from the butterflies which emerge is really rather difficult and is best not attempted if this is a first try. You can let them go wild again but if you want to keep them for a while to watch them, you can do so in a cage like that described for larvae. Give them fresh flowers daily – flowers like buddleia and valerian which have plenty of nectar – and in addition place a pad of cotton wool soaked in weak honey solution on the netting for them to feed from.

Butterflies emerging in cage

BUTTERFLY FAMILIES OF THE WORLD

Satyridae

This family, the browns, occurs in all geographical regions of the world and some of the species are very common indeed. They range in size from not much more than 3 cm to about 10 cm (1 to 4 in) wingspan. They are usually a shade of brown, but sometimes grey. Most species have false eye-spot markings. The larvae are mostly grass feeders and typically have pointed head and tail ends, sometimes with a horn or tail. The pupa is generally suspended but, in some species it is formed on the ground. One or more of the nervures on the fore wing of the butterfly is always dilated, a characteristic of this family. ·

The European Marbled White (*Melanargia galathea*) has the appearance, at first sight, more of the Pieridae but on closer inspection has the characteristics which place it in the Satyridae. This family also includes the Meadow Brown, Ringlet, the erebias from the Alps, the American wood nymphs and the giant *Melanitis leda* which is so common in parts of tropical Asia and Australia.

A satyrid — the Marbled White

Danaidae

This family is confined almost entirely to the tropical regions and its species are most numerous in the Indo-Australian region. Wingspans vary from about 5 cm (2 in) to 17 or 20 cm (7 or 8 in) in a few species of the tree nymphs (*Hestia*) which occur in Malaysia and nearby islands. Probably the most well known species is the Monarch or Milkweed butterfly (*Danaus plexippus*) which occurs in North and South America and has now spread to many Pacific islands as far as Australia and New Guinea and is also found on the Canary Isles.

All species in this family are distasteful to predators and in fact some contain very considerable amounts of lethal poison, which is undoubtedly derived from the larval food-plant. These are very strong butterflies, not easily killed by adverse conditions. They will often recover after being crushed and taken for dead. The males have unique scent brushes which they can extend from the tail during courtship and will do so if caught and held in the hand. The effect is very attractive indeed and is seen especially in species of *Euploea*. The *Euploea* species often have scent 'brands' on the fore wing, horizontal bars of scent scales. In the males of other species, notably in the genus *Danaus,* there is a scent pouch on one of the veins of the hind wing; this is not found in other butterflies.

Danaids fly with a rather slow, almost flapping motion and favour the sunny edges of forests or roadways. They often congregate around pools and waterfalls and fly along river courses. The larvae are gregarious and feed mainly on species of *Asclepias* (milkweed) and *Ficus*. They are conspicuously marked, often in yellow and black, with warning colours. They have fleshy protuberances on the thoracic and tail segments which they can control and voluntarily move with a whipping action.

The pupae hang head downwards from the cremaster. Those of the *Danaus* species are a beautiful pale green with a ring of yellow and metallic spots. The pupae of many species of *Euploea* are silvered and shiny, just like a mirror, and they reflect their background, so they seem to melt away as if transparent. Nearly all species are mimicked by members of other butterfly families.

Danaids — *Danaus plexippus*
from North America,

Parantica sita from Asia

Ithomiidae

A curious group of butterflies which is found, with the exception of one species, only in the Americas. Most species are in the tropical belt and they only extend a little into North America. All are long, narrow-winged butterflies with slender bodies, usually very long and reminiscent of a dragon-fly. Many species have very transparent wings, sometimes with heavy black veining. A number of species are orange and yellow, rather like many of the heliconiids. Ithomiids are related to the danaids and they are distasteful.

An ithomiid — *Thyridia confusa*

Acraeidae

The Acraeidae live almost exclusively in Africa, though one or two species are found in Australia and India. These are characterized by their rather rounded, narrow wings which are often very transparent. Some species are very prettily marked with pink, others are grey and rather dull. They are all small to medium size. Acraeas are not attacked by birds and their protection undoubtedly comes from the larval foodplant, *Passiflora*. Many species are very common.

Heliconiidae

Medium-sized butterflies with very long slender wings. Heliconiids live in tropical America, only one species occurring as far north as the United States. They are extremely numerous and there are many species. Some are very gaily coloured with scarlet, blue and yellow on black.

Heliconiids are renowned for their mimicry of each other and of other families which resemble them in appearance. In fact the mimicry is so effective that it is not always easy to distinguish the species without dissecting the genitalia. One which is normally black with red bands may imitate another species with totally different patterning in orange and yellow. This is a most interesting family to study and a collection of all its species and variations would be very large indeed.

The larvae feed on *Passiflora;* when they first hatch their heads are larger than their bodies. A final instar larva is a magnificent sight with six branching spines on each segment. The chrysalis is peculiarly shaped, angular and covered with projections, looking rather like a shrivelled leaf.

An acraea — *Acraea acrita*

A heliconiid — *Heliconius amaryllis*

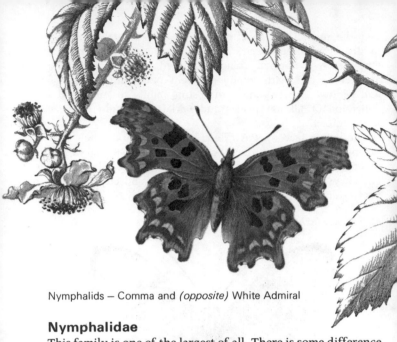

Nymphalids — Comma and *(opposite)* White Admiral

Nymphalidae

This family is one of the largest of all. There is some difference of opinion amongst entomological authors as to just which groups of species should be included in the family Nymphalidae. For instance, some relegate the Danaidae and Satyridae (and other families too) to sub-families of the Nymphalidae, which makes it even larger still. In this book, however, the more generally accepted divisions have been followed and family status has been given to the Danaidae, Satyridae, Heliconiidae, Morphidae, etc. There is no right or wrong way, and classification depends upon a grouping of characteristics which is to some extent arbitrary because there are so many possible combinations.

The European butterflies in this family are the fritillaries, and the genera *Vanessa, Apatura* and *Limenitis*. They are all strong, fast fliers and are fond of sunshine. Many species are common. The purple emperors (*Apatura*) are attracted to carrion and to sweet sap or fruit. The vanessids and notably the Red Admiral and Comma, are also fond of fruit. Flowers sometimes attract numbers of vanessids which are well known

in gardens. The other genera in this family are woodland or meadow species.

In North America, as in Europe, the two main groups of nymphalids are the fritillaries (which include the genera *Melitaea* and *Argynnis*) and the vanessids. Both are very like the European species in appearance but few species are common to both regions. In addition there are a few tropical species which make their way up from central America. The temperate parts of Australia and New Zealand have comparable nymphalids to those in North America and Europe.

In the tropics there is tremendous diversity in this family and some of the species are amongst the world's most beautiful butterflies. The powerful South American *Agrias* spring to mind. These robust butterflies are coloured with the most gorgeous underside patterning. The smaller *Catagramma* butterflies, also in South America, are not unlike miniature *Agrias*. South America is rich in nymphalids, as indeed it is in all butterflies.

The South American species are mostly small to medium in

size and include the iridescent *Doxocopa, Deione, Dryas,* the longtailed *Megalura* and a host of others.

In Africa the prominent genus is *Charaxes,* which is as large and powerful as *Agrias.* There are many species and some are very beautifully marked. They are easily attracted to bait. There are also many pansies (*Precis*) and other smaller genera such as *Phalantha, Neptis, Biblyia* and others which are not unusually bright.

The Asian and Indo-Australian Nymphalidae are very numerous indeed and here only a few of the prominent groups can be mentioned. There are some *Charaxes* and allied *Eriboea* and *Polyura* which are all powerful, robust butterflies. The amazing leaf butterflies (*Kallima*), the numerous but dull *Euthalia* and smaller butterflies such as *Precis, Neptis* and the beautifully marked map butterflies (*Cyrestris*) are also represented in this region. The lacewings (*Cethosia*) are some of the loveliest, prettily edged and marked with reds and oranges and in Asia there are several vanessids. This wide region is also the stronghold of the mimetic *Hypolimnas* species which copy the danaids.

A nymphalid —
the Map Butterfly

A brassolid —
the Owl Butterfly

Brassolidae

The brassolids occur only in Central and South America. By far the majority of species are the owl butterflies (*Caligo* species). These are mostly very large, 15 to 20 cm (6 to 8 in) across and with a large wing area. The uppersides are seldom strongly marked but many have the most attractive shades of iridescent pale blue and violet, subtly mixed with greys and browns. A few are more brightly coloured with bright iridescent blue like the morphos, or with deep orange patches. The underside markings, however, are the striking feature of this family. On the hind wings are two huge eye-like markings, surrounded by a mottled almost feathery pattern which extends to the forewings. A set specimen held upside down bears an extraordinary resemblance to the head and shoulders of an owl. The butterfly, when disturbed, flicks open its wings and jerks them vigorously in a menacing way and undoubtedly intimidates any attacking predator by this means. Other genera include *Opsiphanes* which are smaller and less beautiful, *Euryphanis*, and *Brassolis*, all of which have eye-spots on the underside.

Morphidae

These magnificent butterflies rank with the Indo-Australian *Ornithoptera* or birdwings as being the finest and most spectacular in the world. They live only in Central and South America and the majority occur in the tropical regions of Brazil, Peru, Bolivia and Colombia. The wingspans range from a little over 10 cm (4 in) to around 25 cm (10 in) in the case of one species, *Morpho hecuba*.

Morphos are famous for the incredibly intense iridescent blue that is seen in the males of some of the species. It is a shining, deep blue metallic colour which has to be seen to be appreciated. Not all the *Morpho* species, however, are blue all over like this. At least four species, *hercules, theseus, perseus* and *hecuba,* are mainly brown with suffusions of greenish, silver or orange-brown. These species are, nevertheless, by no means dull, and the giant *hecuba,* banded in bright orange, or blue in the case of form *cisseis,* is a truly splendid sight.

There are three species which are translucent papery white or very pale eau de nil, quite unlike any other butterfly, these are *laertes, catenarius* and *polyphemus.* Then there is a group which we might put loosely under the heading of the '*achilles* group', *Morpho achilles* being the best known of those with this type of colouring which is basically black with a very broad band of iridescent blue or violet running down both the fore and hind wings. In *M.peleides* this band covers most of the wing. The underside of the *achilles* group is beautifully marked with rings and streaks of green and red on black. The species which have the characteristic deep blue include the smaller ones such as *aega, adonis* and *aurora.* *Menelaus* is a little larger than these, about 14 cm (5½ in) in wingspan and it has a much larger form by the name of *nestira.* *Cypris,* from Colombia and Central America, is the brightest of all the morphos and has an attractive contrasting white band across the wings. *Rhetenor* is another brilliant blue species and it has a white banded form called *pseudocypris.* There are some very pretty species which are a pale, opalescent blue. These include *sulkowski* from Colombia, *eugenia* and a magnificent large species *godarti* from Bolivia.

Morpho larvae are hairy and live gregariously.

A morpho – *Morpho menelaus*

Amathusiidae

The amathusiids are medium to very large species which occur only in Asia and Indo-Australia. In relationship they are close to the South American morphos and also have many characteristics in common with the Satyridae.

These butterflies are not sun-loving; they keep to shady forests and fly mainly at dusk or even early at night. They are weak fliers and flap along only short distances at a time. It is not a large family. *Thaumantis* and *Zeuxidia* are brightly marked in iridescent blue and *Stichopthalma camadeva* from India is a lovely lavender blue. But the other species, with the exception of *Taenaris,* are rather dull in colour, though they often have interesting wing shapes. *Taenaris* is a genus of mostly white or pale brown butterflies, marked with very large and conspicuous eye-spots. To see one of these lumbering through a forest clearing is an amusing sight.

The larvae of amathusiids are gregarious and sometimes become serious pests in cocoa plantations. The pupa is usually green, with the head drawn out into two long points.

An amathusiid—
Taenaris catops

Libytheidae

This group is sometimes classified as a subfamily of the Erycinidae. Here it is treated separately because there are a number of separating characteristics, mainly in the genitalia. The most outstanding feature is the way in which the palps on the head are unusually long and protruding, giving the family the popular name of 'beaks'. There are very few species indeed and most are tropical. The basic colour of mouse-brown with markings in orange is common to very nearly all species.

A libytheid —
Libythea celtis celtoides

Erycinidae

This is a family of small butterflies of which there are hundreds of species in South America. Only one, the Duke of Burgundy Fritillary (*Hamearis lucina*), lives in Europe. Certain of the South American erycinids are exceptionally beautiful, being brightly coloured with brilliant shot blues and reds (*Diorina* and *Ancyluris*), greens (*Lyropteryx*) and other pure reds and blues. There are a great many less attractive species but as a whole this is a very attractive and most interesting family to study. The life histories of most species are unknown.

An erycinid —
Ancyluris formosissima

Lycaenidae

This family comprises thousands of species and forms but it can be loosely divided into the coppers, blues and hairstreaks. The coppers are the least numerous: their fiery burnished copper colour is unequalled in any of the other Lepidoptera. In Britain there is now only one species, *Lycaena phlaeas*; the Large Copper (*L. dispar*) has become extinct. In continental Europe, however, there are a score or more of species and forms.

Coppers occur in all geographical regions but they are less numerous in the tropics. The most numerous in all regions are the blues. In Europe the small blue butterflies which swarm on hillsides and chalk downs in summer are well known (though not as common as they used to be). They are subject to great variation and have been given hundreds of variety names by collectors, who sometimes specialize in collecting just one or two species. The males are generally a shade of blue but the females are brown. In Britain there are eight species, but some ten times this number are found in the rest of Europe.

Throughout the world the blues are nearly always quite small, less than 2 cm (1 in) across, indeed the smallest butterflies in the world are blues, but in Africa one or two species are about 6 cm ($2\frac{1}{2}$ in) across. Some of the blues are without any blue colouring and in the tropics many are white with black markings. Many are tailed and could be confused with hairstreaks. The undersides are nearly always marked with rows of tiny spots and rings on a pale background and it is these markings which are subject to such variation, referred to earlier. The blues are often very commonly found in tropical countries. They fly in grassy places at the edges of woodland and in gardens. There are very many species in Asia and Indo-Australia and in Africa they are moderately well represented but there are few lycaenids in South America.

The larvae of the Lycaenidae are shaped rather like a woodlouse. Generally they are a shade of green to match their foodplant. The larvae of blues feed on plants in the family Leguminosae, clovers and vetches as a general rule, though there are exceptions. They attract ants which 'milk' them for a honey-dew secretion produced from glands on the

Two lycaenids —
Adonis Blue *(upper)*
and Continental Large
Copper *(below)*

back. Some species, notably the Large Blue (*Maculinea arion*) actually live in an ants' nest and feed on the ants' larvae.

The third group, the hairstreaks, is very widespread and has some of the world's prettiest butterflies. In Europe they are all small, about 2 cm (1 in) across, but some of the tropical species are three times the size or more. They are tailed and in some cases the tails are long and conspicuous. The colours vary tremendously. In Japan there are species with an overall, iridescent, light bottle-green. Many are shining purples and blues and most have undersides that are quite as attractive as the upperside.

Thecla coronata from Bolivia is nearly 7 cm (3 in) across; the upperside is bright shining blue, edged with black and the underside is exquisitely coloured in iridescent green, barred with maroon and white with markings in black. There are two long, tapering tails on each hindwing. Related species with similar colouring occur throughout the world and the other beautiful *Thecla* species and allied hairstreaks also have jewel-like markings.

The larvae are similar in shape to those of the blues and coppers and the majority feed on leaves of trees, pressed tight against the leaf and camouflaged to match the veining.

A lycaenid — a Japanese hairstreak

A pierid — *Hebomoia glaucippe*

Pieridae

This is a most colourful family of butterflies, characterized by yellow and white but many have, in addition, brilliant patches of reds, oranges, pinks and greens.

In Europe the pierids include the Large White, Brimstone, Orange Tip, clouded yellows and the other whites, and in North America there are American counterparts to these. The clouded yellows are sometimes found high in the Alps and the commoner species, e.g. *Colias croceus* and *Colias hyale* are sometimes found in large quantities and in migratory flights. *Colias croceus* cannot survive the winter in Britain and new migrations each year keep the species going. The same applies to *Colias hyale*, but this is rare in Britain.

The South American Pieridae are mostly rather unlike those in other regions. There is a genus, *Neophasia*, which bears some resemblance to the Bath whites (*Pontia*) of Europe and even by superficial resemblance to the African *Belenois*. There are some true *Pieris* species, including the Small White (*Pieris rapae*). *Perrhybris*, which is an exclusively South American genus whose females are often not white but orange, black and yellow, mimics *Lycorea*, *Mechanitis*, etc. *Pereute* is an unusual group of basically black species and the long-winged *Dismorphia* species are numerous. These are related to *Leptidea* in Europe, the wood whites. In Africa the two outstanding groups are the *Belenois,* referred to earlier, and *Colotis* which remind one of the orange tips but are not closely related. These can be quite large and the colour of the wing tips varies from yellows and oranges to iridescent blues and purples. In Asia and Indo-Australia the Pieridae are very numerous, but perhaps more outstanding are the *Catopsilia* species, small to medium in size and usually a shade of yellow or orange. These are migratory and usually very common. The other more outstanding group is the genus *Delias*. These are the most colourful of the pierids. The upperside is seldom other than black and white but the underside, and in particular the hind wing, is very beautifully marked in bright colours. The giant orange tips (*Hebomoia*) are spectacular with a wingspan of 10 to 12 cm (4 to 5 in). *Ixias* is a common genus in Asia, resembling superficially the clouded yellows, and this is subject to strong natural variation.

A pierid — the Clouded Yellow

Papilio bianor —
a papilionid

Papilionidae

This is a very varied and well known family of butterflies, represented by over 500 species throughout the world. In Britain the Swallowtail (*Papilio machaon*) is the sole representative and in the rest of Europe there are only some half dozen species. A great many species, although loosly termed 'swallowtails', are in fact tail-less and, such is the variation in appearance, that there seems to be no comparison at all between the apollos of the Alps and the giant East Indian birdwings (*Ornithoptera*); nevertheless they are in the same family.

North America has more *Papilio* species than are found in Europe. These include several in the *machaon* species group, the tiger swallowtails and several apollos. These are butterflies with very rounded, often transparent wings, which are basically white, with markings in black and usually red as well. The South American species of Papilionidae are very numerous. They are dominated by those sometimes termed the 'black papilios' which are sometimes marked with brilliant patches of colour on a black background. Other prominent species are the white and black, long-tailed *protesilaus* group and the other 'sword-tail' species which include *thyastes,* a lovely deep-yellow species, *serville* and *leucaspis.* These are just some of the South American groups.

In Africa there are two giant species, *zalmoxis* and *antimachus.* These are as large as birdwings but do not belong to the same tribe. *Antimachus* can be up to 25 cm (10 in) across, with long, very narrow wings. *Papilio* species in Africa are not numerous, though some are common, notably *demodocus, nireus* and *antheus.*

In Asia and Indo-Australia the different groups are numerous and very varied. The sword-tails (*Graphium* species) are common, usually in shades of blue-green on black, some black-barred on white. The *Papilio ulysses* species group of shining blue or green iridescent swallowtails is particularly lovely, so too are the green *paris, crino, buddah* species. But the most fantastic and glorious butterflies in the world are the giant *Ornithoptera.* Some of these are black and yellow, but the rarer species in New Guinea have males which are shining green and golden, turquoise and blue, with very elegant shapes to the wings. Some are exceptionally rare and fetch high prices.

A papilionid – the Swallowtail *Papilio machaon*

Large Skipper —
a hesperiid

Hesperiidae

This family is so completely different in its structure and habits that it is regarded by some as a super-family of its own, of equal status with all other butterflies. The neuration differs, the head is wider than the thorax, and in the flight and resting position (more like a moth) they are unlike other butterflies. There are about thirty species of this family (the skippers), in Europe and only eight in Britain. They occur in all geographical regions. In Europe the average size is around 2 cm (1 in) across but in the tropics they are often twice this size. The number of species runs into thousands. The majority are not brightly coloured, usually a shade of dull brown or orange-brown but there are some colourful exceptions in Asia and especially South America, where several of the species have long sweeping tails. It is in South America that the skippers are best represented. The larvae are usually grass feeders and live in hiding, rolling themselves up in leaves or blades of grass spun together, or in a web of silk. They have a large head, a thin neck and their body tapers at each end.

BUTTERFLY HABITATS AND SEASONS

In the tropical regions

In the tropics butterflies are very numerous indeed, but a visitor to tropical parts for the first time might be surprised to find how hard it is to find butterflies in certain seasons and localities. Ideal places may be found at the edges of forest and in woodland clearings where the butterflies, which fly high above the forest canopy, sometimes come down to feed.

In some parts there is a noticeable lack of flowers, and butterflies often have to find their food from other sources. They are particularly attracted to muddy banks and water seepages in mud, where they sometimes congregate in hundreds over a small patch. Pierids and papilionids in particular congregate like this and they look most spectacular. River banks, waterfalls and even dried up watercourses are all very good localities for butterflies.

There are definite flight passages in certain parts and if you came across one of these and watch for an hour or so, many species will be seen. Many butterflies are attracted to

Butterflies in Malaya feeding on mud

gardens: papilios, nymphalids, pierids and others may be seen in profusion if there are plenty of flowers.

Scrubland in hot countries can be quite productive of commoner species. Sometimes this type of habitat is swarming with little blues, small nymphalids like *Precis,* the grass yellows (*Eurema* species, Pieridae), *Colotis* and others.

In the tropics butterflies generally start flying about 9 a.m. and by 3 p.m. many will be settling for the night. Dusk comes soon after 6 p.m. Amathusiids will be out around this time and a few satyrids, but they are exceptions. Skippers come out at dawn and other species are also constant in their time of appearance, some not emerging until noon or after.

Butterflies may be attracted by bait and this is particularly successful in forest regions. *Charaxes* in Africa and Asia, *Agrias* and *Prepona* in South America all come to bait and it is very often the Nymphalidae which are attracted. The bait can be dung or carrion, but best of all is rotting fruit; banana or pineapple is particularly recommended. To find the early stages, eggs, larvae or pupae, in the tropics it is best to search for the right foodplants but one is often able to find interesting things by random search.

In temperate regions

At the right time of year the most productive types of habitat are the chalk downs and grassy hillsides. Collecting in the Alpes Maritimes, the Jura, the Swiss and Austrian Alps are experiences not to be forgotten. The grassy slopes teem with thousands of blues, sometimes a dozen or more species, skippers, browns and lovely day-flying moths also. In Britain there are fewer species, and indeed nowadays fewer localities where there is such profusion. These types of localities are also very productive in North America and Australia, where, although different species are represented, they usually belong to the same families.

Heaths are sometimes a good place to see butterflies. Again the blues are found, small coppers, sometimes hairstreaks and often certain browns. The *Melitaea* group of fritillaries such as *athalia* sometimes occur also. Open meadows where the grass has not been cut and where flowers abound can be full of butterflies, but pastures and cultivated land seldom have many species unless it is very rough and wild.

In woodlands quite exciting species can be found. The New Forest, for example, has an abundance of the commoner

Collecting on chalk downs

styrids, skippers, certain blues, coppers, the less common hairstreaks, vanessids, brimstones, the larger fritillaries (*Argynnis*), the whites, and two rarities, the Purple Emperor (*Apatura iris*) and the White Admiral (*Limenitis camilla*). Not all woodland is so productive, but it is a very prolific type of habitat. You must search in clearings, along rides and at the edges, rather than deep in the forest. Coniferous woodland is not so productive as deciduous forest.

Gardens attract Nymphalidae, including vanessids such as peacocks, Red Admirals and tortoiseshells in particular, the whites, brimstones, browns, coppers and certain blues. Much depends on the size of the garden and how wild it is. If it is close to wild habitat like woodland it is more likely to be frequented by butterflies than in an area surrounded only by other houses and gardens.

High mountainous regions often have their own particular species. The high Alps, Himalayas, Andes, and the mountainous areas of South-west Asia, for example, have their own species of *Apollo, Colias, Erebia, Argynnis* and *Lycaena*. Some very rare species occur at high altitudes.

Butterfly seasons

In warm countries and the tropics butterflies are often continuously brooded, that is to say they breed continuously without any period of diapause. This is as one would imagine since there is neither winter nor seasons as we know them. It is therefore surprising to find that the majority of species are in fact seasonal and certain times of the year are better than others for butterflies. The best flight season in tropical America is from November to February, coinciding with similar periods in South Africa, southern Australia and New Zealand. In Africa the best seasons are dependent on latitude and in northern India they are, as in northern and central Europe, June to September. The Asian monsoon seasons have a great bearing on butterfly flight seasons. The fierce dry seasons produce special forms in many species, often smaller than the wet season form, and butterflies at this time are far less prolific. Some species are not on the wing at all during the dry season.

In temperate countries there are no winter butterflies and the main flight season is generally from May or June until September. In the Mediterranean and other warmer parts, the season is a good deal longer, starting as early as February. The Speckled Wood (Satyridae), Holly Blue and Small Copper are three examples of butterflies which have from two to four appearances during the summer and the number is sometimes dependent on climate. In Europe the first butterflies to appear are those which awake from hibernation. Usually the first seen is the Brimstone often as early as February. Peacocks and tortoiseshells follow in March and April, together with Speckled Woods later in April. May brings out the first lycaenids, some browns, and early fritillaries, and in June the season is well under way with dozens of species flying. This continues until early September when there are fewer species about, though the vanessids are very much in evidence. The season barely straggles on through September and in October and November only a few late individuals are found. The only butterflies found in winter would be those awoken from hibernation or ones that hibernate late.

Collecting in the tropics

COLLECTING EQUIPMENT AND METHODS

Collecting equipment should be kept as simple and compact as possible. The net is the first essential. Decide whether you are going to need one which will fold for convenience in carrying. Collapsible nets must have a rigid frame which will not fold on you at a crucial moment! Most net frames are round but the Kite Net, with a frame shaped like a kite, has a lot to commend it. The frame is larger, the bag deeper and many prefer its shape. For high flying species obviously a long-handled net has advantages, but it is very unwieldy. Without a handle the net is more easily manipulated; a fairly short handle is probably the best compromise. Black netting is easier to see through than other colours; the material should be soft and transparent.

Next, you want something to put your catch in. Living butterflies travel well in cardboard pill boxes, one to a box. A small satchel is needed to carry these unless you have large pockets. A killing jar should be fairly small and two can be useful. A bottle charged with potassium cyanide is very effective, but this is a dangerous poison and not recommended for children. The alternative is to use a killing fluid, ethyl acetate, chloroform, etc., poured onto absorbent material in the jar. This can evaporate too fast in hot weather and care must be taken not to let the specimens get too wet. Alternatively, one can use a syringe and one of the killing fluids mentioned above. You insert the needle of the syringe into the thorax between the legs and inject a minute amount of fluid.

Making a paper storage envelope

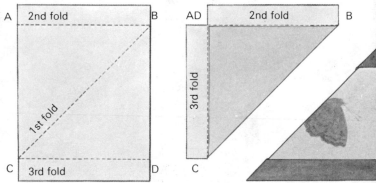

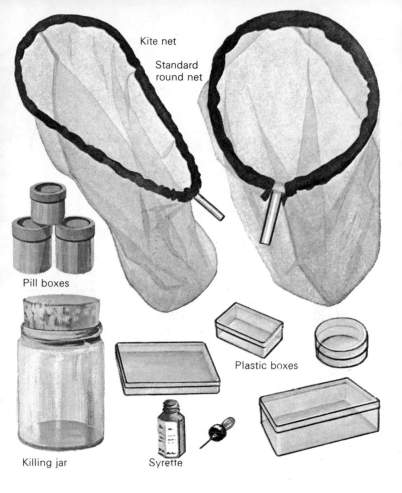

Kite net

Standard round net

Pill boxes

Plastic boxes

Killing jar   Syrette

The dead specimen can be put immediately into a triangular paper envelope which is folded as shown in the diagram opposite. These 'papered' specimens, can be stored in a flat tin. Simpler than a syringe is a 'syrette' which is simply a bottle with a needle and bulb inserted into the cap. It is carried, ready charged and available for use at any time. To collect larvae or eggs, some simple tins or plastic boxes are required and a few paper bags are especially useful.

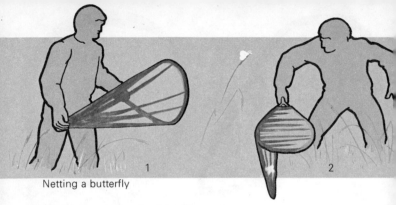
Netting a butterfly

How to use a butterfly net

There is nothing complicated about the use of a butterfly net. Basically there are two methods of approach. The first is for a butterfly settled on a flower or foliage; the second is for a butterfly that is flat on the ground or sitting on a flat wall.

In the first case, approaching from behind if possible, stalk gently, making sure that your shadow will not fall on the butterfly when you are close. Hold the net in one hand and with the other, hold the very end of the net bag like a balloon (1). Like this you have absolute control of the net. Get to within a short distance and, at an opportune moment, make a firm sideways sweep of the net, engulfing not only the butterfly, but the flowerhead as well. The next important step is to sweep the net through the air so that the butterfly goes deep into the bag and, while sweeping, flick the end of the bag over the edge of the frame so that it is folded with the butterfly inside (2).

A butterfly resting on the ground is approached in a similar way but with the bag held vertically (3). When you bring the net down over the butterfly, keep the net bag extremity held high and the frame hard on the ground. The butterfly will then fly to the top and the net can be deftly turned and folded over (4). When catching a butterfly in flight, sweep it deep into the net and twist the end over the frame as described earlier.

To remove the butterfly from the net, take a pill box. Remove the lid and with the base capture the specimen inside the net bag. If you hold the box with the transparent base to

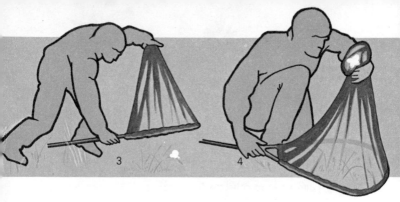

the sky, the butterfly will fly to the light and the lid can be put on, inside the net, without the butterfly escaping. Inspect the specimen and don't kill it before you are sure it is one that you will keep.

You will probably find places locally where you can find butterflies in the right season, but when you have collected for a while you may wish to get species which live in different types of habitat. Standard reference books will usually indicate the seasons and habitats of a particular species.

Removing a butterfly from the net using a pill box

Using a paper bag to collect wild larvae

Take the equipment you need and with luck and good judgment you will find what you are looking for. A lot of fun can be had from looking for the early stages. Caterpillars are probably the easiest to find. A paper bag makes a surprisingly efficient collecting receptacle. It folds flat when not required and if you find species like Peacock or Tortoiseshell larvae, which do not cling but curl up and drop from the plant, you can hold the open bag beneath the plant and shake them in. Screw the neck up tightly! You can buy a sweep net which you use to sweep grass and foliage for larvae; actually a kite net can also be used if you are careful. Be sure that you know what the larvae feed on before you take them home. Similarly you can find larvae by beating bushes and trees with a stick over an outspread kite net or a sheet carried for the purpose.

The larvae found by beating and sweeping are very often those of moths, but are just as interesting to rear.

Looking for Orange Tip eggs

A more specific search can also be very fruitful. If, for instance, you know of a colony of White Letter Hairstreak (*Thecla w-album*) on wych elm, or suspect that there could be a colony, search the leaves from beneath the tree and the dark silhouettes of the larvae can be seen against the sky. Brimstone eggs can be found on the terminal shoots of buckthorn and you can search for the little orange eggs of the Orange Tip on the flower heads of garlic mustard. By reading about the habits of each species you will be guided as to how and where to search for a particular species. Some are extraordinarily well camouflaged; certain larvae are countershaded so that they melt into their backgrounds and are easily missed even with the most careful search. European butterfly examples have been cited here but the same principles apply in any part of the world. If literature is not available, then there can be an even greater incentive to discover something for yourself, which will also be a useful record for others.

Camouflage — Leaf Butterfly *(upper)* Orange Tip Larva *(lower)*

MAKING A REFERENCE COLLECTION

The purpose of a collection

There is a natural instinct to collect beautiful things, and butterfly collectors are sometimes accused of collecting just for the sake of amassing a collection. There is justification for concern about collecting, especially in areas where butterflies are becoming scarcer, but some conservationists condemn all collecting, whatever the reason. Moderation is the best policy in most things and above all common sense should be used. If a species is scarce then only a few examples should be taken, and great thought should be given before killing a healthy female which would otherwise help to propagate the species. A rare species should not be taken. A net is itself not a lethal weapon and is just as necessary to obtain specimens for breeding as for a collection.

Cabinet layouts

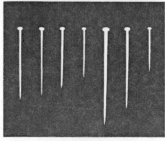

A reference collection usually represents the range of species from an area, a group or family of species, or a range of variation. You will probably find that your interest starts to follow a definite course and you will eventually build up on that course. It is not wise to attempt to build a collection of the world's butterflies – there are too many! A reference collection helps you to study a group of species intelligently and even first class colour illustrations are not a substitute for the real thing.

It is likely that you will want to start collecting the more attractive species, but even the less attractive ones are fascinating when you come to study them in greater depth. Unless you are a variety hunter, there is no need to have drawers full of a species. Generally it is necessary only to have two pairs of a species, with one pair set as undersides, but in addition you may need to add geographical and seasonal varieties if they occur in that species. Arrange the specimens in rows vertically, with

(Top) Continental pins *(upper)* and English pins *(lower)*
(Left) Continental *(upper)* and English *(lower)* pins in use

the name of the species at the bottom of the row, as illustrated. Some collectors put the family and generic names at the head of the column, with only the species name below the column; this is a matter of choice. But above all, make sure that the species are clearly labelled and that each pin bears, beneath the specimen, a data label stating when, where and by whom it was caught. Altitude is a further useful item of information relating to species distribution.

Equipment needed

Entomology is rather beset by conventions. Many of these are as the result of experience, but there is no reason why a collector cannot modify or invent new methods and equipment both for preparing and laying out his collection to his liking. The main essential is that the collection should be accompanied by proper data and should help him learn a little more about the subject.

Butterfly cabinets with glass topped drawers are generally used to house a collection, but double-sided wooden store-boxes are also sold for this purpose and are a cheaper alternative. The English style of pinning differs in that pins of different lengths are used according to the size of the specimen. This gives a neat appearance and the pins are unobtrusive but the Continental pins have other advantages ('Continental' pins are in fact used universally). They are all the same length, about 3 cm (1½ in), but they vary in thickness. Specimens are all set at the same level, regardless of size and there is enough space on the pin beneath the insect to have several data labels. The main disadvantages are that they are springy and sometimes cause damage, and that the setting boards and deeper drawers required are rather more expensive.

You will need to decide on the type of container that will house your collection and also the method of pinning. Then obtain from an entomological supplier the necessary pins,

Entomological forceps

setting boards, setting strips, needle and entomological forceps. These forceps are curved and ideally suited to handling both papered and pinned, set specimens. They are particularly useful for handling specimens which are to be relaxed prior to setting. This relaxing process is only necessary if the specimens have dried out after being caught or have been papered for some time. Relaxing puts moisture back into the muscles and makes the wings supple for setting. A relaxing box has an absorbent material which is soaked in relaxing fluid. Specimens are put in, on a paper lining and left for about eight to ten hours in a warm cupboard. The forceps are then used to break the stiffness of the wings before the specimen is put on to the setting board. There are other methods, including the use of crushed laurel leaves, but the relaxing fluid method is very sound. Do not leave butterflies in a moist atmosphere for more than a day or so or mould will appear.

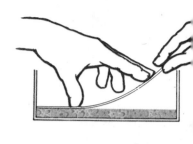

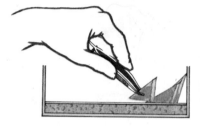

Relaxing butterflies prior to setting

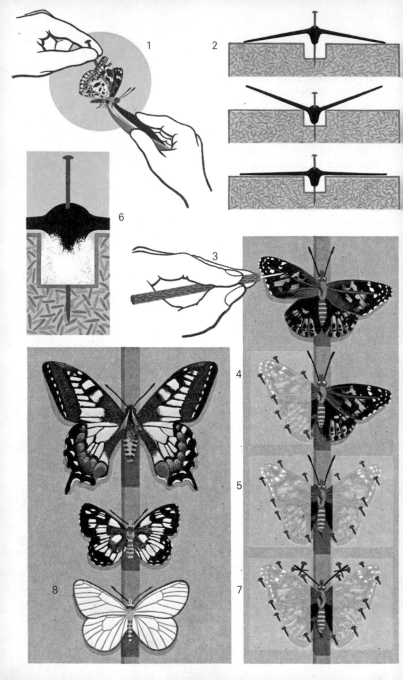

Setting butterflies

Setting is an art which improves with practice. The quickest way to become a good setter is to learn to recognize the faults in your own setting, then there is seldom difficulty in putting them right if you can spot them.

Take a relaxed specimen and pin vertically straight through the thorax (1). Pressure on either side of the thorax with forceps will open the wings to allow this. The pin should not lean in any direction, it should be vertical. Next pin the specimen centrally into the groove of the setting board (2). The specimen must be exactly straight. The thorax must not be too low on the pin or the wings will rise vertically and bend at the point when they are flattened either side of the body. Position the thorax so that the wings lie exactly level on the flat surfaces either side of the groove. Get this right before proceeding, because the next stage prevents further adjustment of level on the pin, without causing damage. Use a setting needle to edge the left fore wing forward, so that the hind edge lies at right angles to the body (3). *This is important.* The point of the needle is gently pushed against a main vein near the leading edge, but try not to pierce the wing. Pin the setting strips over the fore wing and bring up the hind wing in the same way, with the needle point. The gap between the wings should be as illustrated and is slightly dependent on the shape of the wings. This gap is a matter of preference, but try not to make it too large or too small. When you are satisfied, pin the wings into position (4). You may find that this has caused the body to skew on the pin. This can be prevented by putting a pin vertically into the groove, tight against the body on the left side, before moving the wings. The wings on the right hand side are moved into position next (5). (It makes no difference if you prefer to do the right side first.) The body may need to be pinned into a straight position and if it is drooping into the groove, support it on a small pad of cotton wool so that it lies horizontally (6). Finally the antennae are set. Use enough pins to hold the antennae in position so that they run in a v-shape on a parallel with the wings (7). After a suitable period for drying out the specimen is then set (8).

Stages in setting a butterfly. Numbers in the illustration refer to numbered stages in the text.

BREEDING BUTTERFLIES

There are no hard and fast rules about breeding butterflies and a great deal relies on trial and error mixed with common sense. This chapter is designed to help would-be breeders by outlining methods used at the present time but undoubtedly new ways will continue to be found. Most butterflies are not too difficult to rear from the egg or larva stage, but the difficulty comes with trying to get them to pair and lay eggs. Butterflies are fastidious and need the presence of living foodplant. We will, however, start on the assumption that eggs are available to start the cycle.

Whether you have been fortunate in finding some eggs or have obtained them from a butterfly breeder, they may either be loose or on small fragments of withered foodplant, or still attached to growing plants. It is generally agreed that it is easier to rear successfully on growing plants than with living eggs and larvae kept in boxes. But as the latter is often necessary it is a good thing to know how to go about this method.

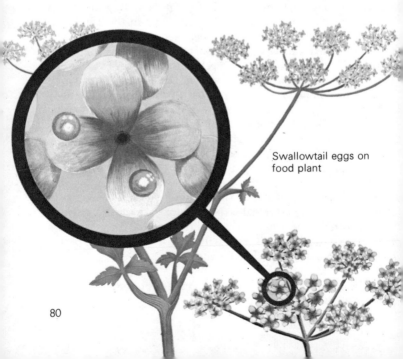

Swallowtail eggs on food plant

Eggs are best kept in a small, transparent plastic box. Sunlight is harmful to boxed livestock so keep the boxes in a north-facing room. The eggs may well darken just before hatching. Let the newly hatched larvae feed on their egg-shells for a while and then transfer them to fresh food. This can either be done by picking them up gently on the tip of a soft paint brush or by putting in a small amount of their foodplant (just for about an hour) and transferring this when they have crawled up on to it. If you have a pot of the correct growing foodplant available it would be as well to transfer the young larvae straight on to this. If not, then use a larger plastic box, approx. 17 × 12 × 5 cm (7 × 5 × 2 in), line it with paper and put freshly cut food on top of the paper lining.

Eggs which are already on growing foodplant can be kept in the sun but if they are in a greenhouse, the temperature should not become much hotter than 32 to 37°C (90 to 100°F). Until the larvae hatch there is no need to cover the plant at all, but if it is caged or put into a fine netting sleeve there is less danger of small spiders, earwigs, etc. eating the eggs. These creatures

Clouded Yellow eggs on clover
kept in a plastic box

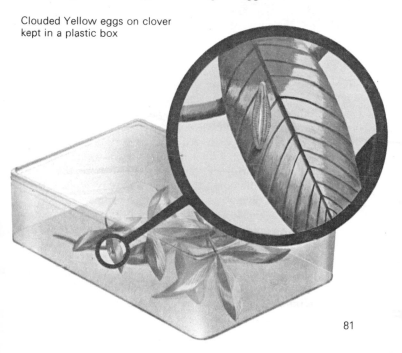

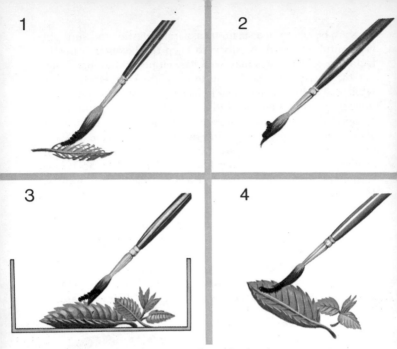

Moving very young larvae on a fine paint brush

are sometimes a problem with potted plants because they can hide so easily at the foot of the plant or the edges of the pot.

The majority of butterfly eggs will hatch within a few days or up to three weeks of being laid. The eggs of overwintering species would normally be laid in the late summer, and in the wild state remain in position on the twig, where they were laid, right through the winter, exposed to all weathers, until they hatch in the spring. If you have some of these, they keep quite well in a plastic box if they are in a very cool place, even in a refrigerator. Bring out the eggs in the spring and watch them carefully, every day, for hatching. The eggs of many *Thecla* and *Lycaena* species hibernate in this way and the newly hatched larvae are minute. They are easily overlooked. If, by misfortune, your eggs hatch before the buds of the foodplant have opened, as a temporary measure you can dissect some buds and feed the tiny pieces of leaf to the larvae. The larvae will sometimes even burrow into the bud.

Stages in cleaning out larvae

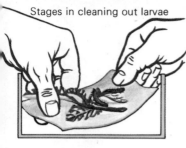

Remove liner and contents

Cut round larvae
Replace larvae on new liner

Add fresh food

Transferring the newly hatched larvae on a soft paintbrush is a gentle method which causes the larvae no harm. Do not try and use it as a brush and sweep the larvae out as this can hurt them. Select dry fresh, clean food that is free from aphis honeydew. Take a reasonable length and arrange it in the box in a bowed fashion so that it is not lying flopped on the bottom but is accessible to larvae even if they wander all round the box. Similarly, do not put an odd leaf or two on the bottom and hope the larvae will not stray from it. It is possible to cram too much food into a plastic box, so be moderate. Clean the boxes out daily, renewing the food at the same time. Remove the paper liner and all the contents. Put in a new liner. The larvae go in next but do not remove them from the leaves and twigs on which they are resting. Cut round them, removing as much old food as possible, and finally put the fresh food in on top of the larvae which will crawl up to it. Make sure that the boxes are not kept in the sun at all.

Plastic boxes are useful because they enable you to control the larvae better than with any other method. In a cage there is a danger that they might escape through a crevice or through the netting. Even in a sound cage they might also wander from the foodplant and starve. Bearing this in mind, once the larvae have grown to about the third instar, it is often better to transfer them to a cage. The cylinder type of cage is very successful and the larvae inside are easily observed. Ventilation is through a gauze panel in the lid. As with plastic boxes this type of cage is not suitable for a sunny position because condensation builds up on the sides and the cage becomes too wet. For small quantities of larvae the miniature cylinder cages sold under the name of 'crystal palaces' or plant propagators are ideal, as also are the larger rectangular sizes. The most satisfactory, though more expensive, type of cage is made with a wooden frame and panels of netting. This is not only suitable for larvae but for pupae and adults. It can also be stood in a greenhouse and in the sun.

Potted food is far more satisfactory than cut food. It is better for the larvae and also less troublesome because the food requires changing far less frequently. If cut food

Plastic cylinder cage

Crystal palaces

Wooden cage

is used, stand it in a jar of water and against one side so that larvae can crawl up again if they fall. The foodplant ought to be changed once every three or four days even if it still looks fresh and is not finished. If you stand a pot of fresh food beside the old, most of the larvae will transfer themselves. The next day the old food can be removed and the few remaining larvae clipped off by hand.

Clean out the cage daily if possible and remove any dead or obviously unhealthy larvae, though don't mistake those which are motionless because they are changing their skins. These must not be pulled off their silk pads. Sleeving is a method which can be very successful if intelligently applied. A sleeve is a bag made of fine cheese-cloth, organdie, or mosquito netting, according to the requirement. A sleeve over a potted foodplant makes a very economical cage and it can be used indoors or out. For very small larvae on a young, tender plant, the lightweight, soft organdie is best. Indoors, when you want

Fresh food placed beside old — the larvae transfer themselves.

to see inside the sleeve, the open netting sleeve (black) is most suitable as long as the larvae are not too small. Out of doors sleeves can be tied over a complete plant, a small tree or just over a branch, with the larvae free inside, living on the fresh growing plant as in the wild state. The white cheese-cloth sleeves are generally used outside, but the black netting sleeves give better air circulation and they do not get so damp. Birds can peck through the netting sleeves and this is why the white is more generally used. Using a double sleeve can prevent this nuisance from birds, but not always. In a spell of really wet and cold weather larvae do not do well in sleeves and are better brought indoors. Never crowd larvae, unless they are a gregarious species, as this often leads to disease. The foodplant must never become stripped of its leaves because if the larvae suffer even partial starvation this weakens them. They will almost certainly die at a later date by catching a disease.

Sleeves of larvae in a hedgerow

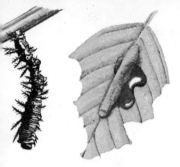

Virused larvae — typical symptoms

Parasites of larvae —

Tachinid fly

Ichneumonid wasp

Braconid *(Apanteles glomeratus)*
Cocoons on Large
White larva

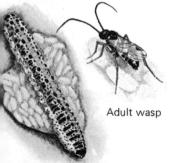

Adult wasp

Parasites and diseases

In captivity parasites are seldom a problem to the breeder. Parasites are either dipterous flies or wasp-like creatures of the order Hymenoptera. They lay their eggs either on the skin of a caterpillar or inject eggs into the caterpillar with a sharp ovipositor. These develop and produce either a multitude of tiny flies or maybe only one, but the result is certain death to the caterpillar. Freshly formed pupae, especially of vanessids and papilionids are sometimes attacked in captivity by little braconid wasps if the larvae are left out in the open.

Diseases caused by viruses and bacteria are a worse problem and little is known about them. The larva hangs limply or lies in a pool of liquid. Sometimes the faeces become very liquid. The causes are generally overcrowding, damp or unclean conditions, wet food, starvation or a number of factors which weaken the caterpillar. It can seldom be cured and spreads easily. Weak sodium hydroxide solution kills viruses and should be used for washing out cages and boxes either as a precaution or after an outbreak.

Pupating conditions for larvae

It is best not to let larvae pupate in plastic boxes as they will become difficult to clean out each day. Large larvae, if not already caged, are best transferred as soon as they show signs of settling down to pupate. If they pupate in sleeves the pupae can either be collected up and put into a cage ready for emergence, or they can be left in the sleeve to emerge if they are not too crowded. In bad weather this is risky and specimens could be spoilt when they are emerging.

Larvae being reared in a cage can really be left to pupate in peace. Depending on the species, they may pupate hanging from the roof of the cage, amongst the foodplant or they may be species which make a chrysalis on the bottom of the cage. Moth larvae need more special attention at this stage if they are a species which burrow into soil to pupate, but butterfly larvae do not do this. As mentioned on the last page, there is a danger from parasites with some butterfly larvae at the time when the pupal skin is still soft; and if the larvae are being kept out of doors, in a greenhouse and anywhere else at all exposed, the large larvae need to be taken indoors, just before they start to spin their web to pupate on.

A successful method is to put up to about twenty into an old shoe box where they settle down quite happily to pupate in safety. It is not a good thing to remove pupae from their secure silk pads unless you have to. The pads give them the anchorage they need and, unless you are very careful, there is a great danger of the pupa breaking and this will inevitably kill it.

Storing pupae for the winter

Pupae need to be kept cool during the winter and it is necessary to prevent them from drying out. In the natural state pupae are regularly moistened by dew and rain and are in exposed conditions where they are generally kept cool. They keep very well in the sealed conditions of plastic boxes or even tins and do best if they are kept in a very cool outhouse. If you can manage to keep them in a refrigerator this is ideal and there is no fear of their becoming too cold. Pupae can withstand temperatures well below freezing. Putting pupae into plastic boxes for the winter contradicts what has been said earlier about not

Pupae form on the roof and floor of the cage and on the foodplant itself.

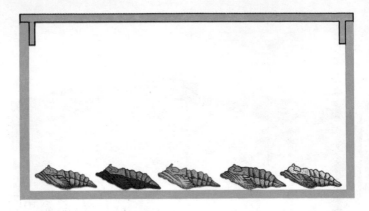

Pupae stored for the winter in a plastic box

removing pupae from the position where they pupated. If the pupae are going to emerge within a few weeks this still applies, but hibernating species of pupae come through the winter more successfully in a closed air-tight container, so it is worthwhile carefully removing them. Those which are attached to twigs can still be cut off on the twig and not be disturbed, but be careful not to put green material in as this goes mouldy and could kill the pupae in the box. Make sure you know the normal time of emergence of the pupae and bring them out of the cold about three weeks early, unless you deliberately want to retard them. Retarding can only be done to some extent and pupae will sometimes emerge at the right season regardless of the low temperature.

If you want to try and make overwintering pupae emerge out of season, this can sometimes be done. Swallowtails, for instance, can be brought out in January instead of May. It is necessary to break the diapause (dormant state) by giving them a 'false winter' in a refrigerator for 6 to 8 weeks. Then bring them into a warmer temperature, gradually increasing it to approximately 22°C (74°F). Emergence will take place within 2 to 3 weeks.

When pupae are ready to be laid out for emergence, use a wooden cage with netting sides, or improvise with a suitable cardboard box. But be sure that you do not use a plastic or metal container, because the sides are too slippery for the emerging butterfly to grip when it climbs up to dry its wings. It is best if all four sides of the cage can be covered with netting and it is also highly desirable that the top should be netting also. When keeping moth pupae it is best to put a layer of peat or pupating material on the bottom of the cage. This can be kept moist and produces the right conditions. With butterflies this moisture is a good thing too, but not essential and there is a slight danger that the butterflies' legs cannot take a proper grip. If this proves to be the case, the best alternative is a sheet of corrugated paper on the bottom, with the pupae lying in the corrugation. This gives an excellent grip. Put in a number of branching twigs 15 cm (6 in) or more high, standing amongst the pupae and leading to the sides of the cage. It is not advisable to stand the cage in sunlight as this is too drying. Use a fine garden spray with tepid water about once a day, more often in really hot weather. This gives the pupae the moisture they need.

Pupae in a cage ready for emergence

Pairing conditions for butterflies

Having successfully emerged as butterflies the next stage is the most difficult and will rely a great deal on ingenuity and experimenting. Butterflies are fastidious and will not always react as expected or hoped for. It is not always enough to re-create natural conditions on the assumption that these will be the most successful. For instance one might consider that Peacocks would be most likely to breed if a whole nettle patch could be covered with a big aviary-type of cage, which would allow them space, height and growing foodplant in the most natural conditions possible. In fact it is generally found that the butterflies will not dip down to lay their eggs as they do in the wild; they are more intent on escape or flying near the roof.

In captivity it seems necessary to tempt butterflies into pairing and egg-laying by having the larval foodplant and the flowers from which they feed, so arranged that both are about 7 cm (3 in) from the cage top and spaced so that the butterflies cannot help bumping into both the flowers and foodplant wherever they fly. This is simply a general principle and undoubtedly certain species will prove to be exceptions.

Artificial hand-pairing is a technique that breeders often find successful and may prove to be the answer to pairing a good many species, if it is developed a little. A fresh pair of butterflies is taken with wings closed, one in each hand. Hold the thorax gently but firmly so that the legs cannot freely move, the wings are tightly held but so that the butterfly is not suffering obvious discomfort. The two abdomens are brought together and after a little stroking the male should open his claspers (which hold the female's abdomen during copulation). Similarly the female should react and by holding the two in the correct position they will join. Next hang the female from the top of a netting cage or a firm twig, with the male hanging free with legs in mid air. Try not to disturb them and after an hour, or several hours, they will part of their own accord. This method works particularly well with the Papilionidae and certain Pieridae and it is worth trying with any species.

Adults emerging in a cage

Butterflies can be sleeved over a foodplant to pair and lay but in an ordinary sleeve they tend to get caught in the folds and trapped until they eventually die. It is necessary to use a modified sleeve as a pairing cage, with a flat, round top (as illustrated). Suspend the pairing cage over the plant and make sure that the leaves are close to the top, together with fresh flowers. Sometimes butterflies will prefer one situation to another with no obvious reason, but if you find that a particular spot in the garden or greenhouse suits a species best, take advantage of it and go on using this position. A pairing cage is suitable for species like the Small Copper or Marsh Fritillary which lay on low-growing plants. Pot up the foodplant (in these cases sorrel and scabious respectively) and tie the bottom of the pairing cage firmly round the pot. The cage can be suspended at such a height as is necessary according to the height of the plant. Some flowers in a jar of water must also be included and changed daily as the butterflies soon use the nectar.

Pairing cage suitable for laying Swallowtails

A wooden cage, covered with netting provides the conditions necessary for many species. The size depends a little on the size of the butterflies. A cage measuring 45 × 45 × 60 cm (18 × 18 × 24 in) is large enough for all but the largest butterflies but for the smaller species, such as the Marsh Fritillary, a cage smaller than this would be better unless you have thirty or forty all together. Use growing food when possible and provide plenty of flowers, both the correct height from the top of the cage. On really hot days the cage can be stood outside with perhaps a windbreak of polythene fixed up, if it is very breezy. Otherwise stand the cage in front of a sunny window or in a greenhouse. The temperature in the greenhouse should not get above 30°C (86°F) if possible, as this weakens the butterflies and they will die much sooner. As with the pairing cage you will find that certain positions and certain greenhouses work better than others, and it is difficult to put

An alternative layout for egg-laying butterflies

one's finger on the reason for this. In addition to flowers some butterflies will feed from fruit, especially if it is a little fermented. Even sections of apple freshly cut can be used.

Another alternative arrangement for pairing is in a round tub. A little while ago it was possible to obtain round wooden cheese tubs about 45 cm (18 in) in diameter. These are ideal but they can be made with a solid round base with hardboard curled round and fastened with nails. An easier alternative is to use the round hat boxes obtainable from some hat shops. These are about 30 cm (12 in) in diameter and very slightly oval. Cut a piece of netting a good deal larger than the size of the top and tie it over using a firm slip knot. The foodplant is arranged inside, together with flowers and the butterflies released inside to pair and lay. This works well with Orange Tips, fritillaries, vanessids and a good many others. An additional method of feeding is with a pad of cotton wool soaked in sugar or honey solution. Take a jam jar and pour in about $\frac{1}{2}$ cm ($\frac{1}{4}$ in) of honey. Fill up with warm water and shake well to mix. Then dip in the cotton wool. Replenish daily, or simply moisten the pads, as the sweetness remains in the pad even when the water has evaporated.

Conditions suitable for egg-laying

The conditions for egg-laying are really much the same as for pairing, but although it is possible to pair some butterflies artificially they will only lay fertile eggs of their own accord. Sunshine is an essential both for pairing and egg-laying, so choose a sunny position. It seldom helps to provide a large space for egg-laying and often they are induced to lay better in a confined space, where the presence of their foodplant stimulates them to keep laying. A female may lay her batch all at once or a few eggs every so often over a week or two. Females sometimes show a preference for one particular shoot or flowerhead and if this is observed, be careful not to move this particular piece of plant as she may smother it with eggs, but hardly lay elsewhere. Make sure that the females are well fed and if you think they are not feeding well enough naturally, place them on the fresh flowers by hand. You will see the proboscis probing the flower if it is feeding. If not, take a long needle and uncurl the proboscis gently until it starts feeding.

Conditions suitable for egg laying in the Silver-washed Fritillary Normally the female lays her eggs on the bark of oak trees, but in captivity this presents a problem. In a tub she will lay quite happily on a double layer of netting which can be folded up and stored for the winter until the larvae (which hatch and hibernate without feeding) awake in the spring.

You can also hand-feed with honey pads. Hold the wings gently but firmly and uncurl the proboscis so that the tip is on the pad. Let the legs rest on the pad as well because they are more at ease like this and they taste through the feet. Comma and Painted Lady butterflies lay very well in a tub if there is a healthy pot of food in with them. Cut food can be used but is not so successful and may wilt quickly. A useful tip for Silver-washed Fritillaries, which normally lay on oak bark, is that they will lay in a tub if you put a double layer of netting over the top. Just give them flowers, no green food. Collect up the netting and store in a plastic box until the hibernated larvae are ready to feed. By experimenting you will find out methods like these for yourself and with a great many tropical species this is necessary, because little or nothing is known of their life histories. If you have the right plants there is little to stop anyone from rearing exciting, tropical species in temperate countries. *Passiflora,* for instance, grows easily and is the food of many tropical Nymphalidae.

It is not easy to obtain livestock of many tropical species but some are available from butterfly breeders or perhaps you might have a friend in the tropics. Many tropical *Papilio* species will feed on *Citrus* plants so this too is useful to grow.

Feeding butterflies

Certain flowers are more attractive to butterflies than others. A useful guide to those which are suitable is to watch on a fine day whether bees are attracted in great numbers. Very often these flowers will also attract butterflies. Flowers in the family Compositae are very often useful. Particular examples are thistle, dandelion, michaelmas daisy and most other daisies. Buddleia, valerian, phlox, *Sedum spectabile,* honesty, sweet william, lavender, wall flower, golden rod, sweet rocket and catmint are all further examples. Some colourful flowers like dahlias or roses are not very often visited by butterflies.

It sometimes helps to sprinkle the flowers with a weak solution of honey or sugar. To make this pour about $\frac{1}{2}$ cm ($\frac{1}{4}$ in) of honey or icing sugar into the bottom of a jam jar. Fill up with warm water and shake well. This solution can also be fed in the form of 'honey pads'.

BUTTERFLIES OF THE DIFFERENT GEOGRAPHICAL REGIONS

In this section will be found illustrations of a representative selection of butterflies, together with brief texts, to give an indication of the different species found in each of the geographical regions selected. The boundaries of these regions are arbitrary and there is overlap of the fauna in these areas. But there are definite geographical points where the fauna and flora start to change owing to altitude, climate or other circumstances.

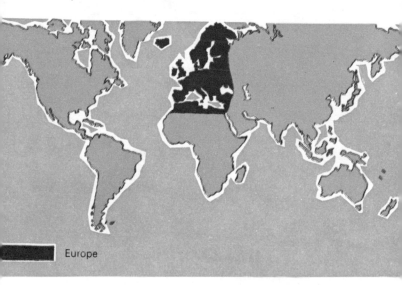

Europe

Europe

The European butterfly fauna overlaps into North Africa as far as the Sahara desert and of course includes the fauna occurring in Spain and other Mediterranean countries. To the east it extends beyond Moscow where it mingles with the colder Asiatic fauna. In Scandinavia the species found correspond much with those in central Europe with the addition of some Arctic species in the far north. The British species are found also in other parts of continental Europe.

1 Northern Brown
2 Purple Emperor
3 Speckled Wood
4 Peacock
5 Silver-washed Fritillary
6 Marsh Fritillary

The Northern Brown (*Erebia aethiops*) is a mountain species of the Satyridae which is very common in most of the Alps and in parts of Scandinavia, but is very local in Scotland and northern England. It flies from July to September. The markings are very variable, and the underside ground colour is especially so. The larva feeds on grasses. The wingspan is about 3 cm (1½ in).

The Speckled Wood (*Pararge aegeria*) is a very common satyrid in and around woodland areas throughout Europe but is less so at high altitudes and colder regions. A form with orange spotting is especially common in the extreme south. This species is seasonally dimorphic. The larva feeds on coarse grasses. It has a wingspan of approximately 3 cm (1½ in).

The Silver-washed Fritillary (*Argynnis paphia*) is in the family Nymphalidae. It is principally a woodland and forest species and is found in mid-summer on bramble blossom and thistle heads. It is common throughout Europe and across northern Asia. A less common female form, *valezina* is silvery grey. The larva feeds on dog violet. The wingspan is nearly 7 cm (3 in).

The Purple Emperor (*Apatura iris*) is a magnificent species of the Nymphalidae, which is rare in England but common in central Europe in oak woods. Only the male has the purple flush. Both larva and pupa very much resemble the leaves of the foodplant, sallow. It is a powerful flier and is attracted to carrion and sweet sap, etc. Its wingspan is over 6 cm (2½ in).

The Peacock (*Nymphalis io*) is another nymphalid and is common throughout Eurasia across to Japan. Generally it is single-brooded in Europe and is sometimes migratory. It is often seen in gardens, orchards and meadows. The larvae are gregarious and feed on stinging nettles. The butterfly makes a curious 'hissing' sound as it moves its wings. The wingspan is approximately 5 cm (2 in).

The Marsh Fritillary (*Euphydryas aurinia*) is a widespread nymphalid, found throughout Europe but is common only in widely dispersed localities and favours chalk hills and marshy ground where its foodplant, scabious, grows. This species is subject to geographical variation. The butterflies tend to remain within their breeding ground. The wingspan is about 3 cm (1½ in).

Duke of Burgundy Fritillary

Common Blue

The Duke of Burgundy Fritillary (*Hamearis lucina*) is not in fact a fritillary although marked like one. It is the only European representative of the Nemeobïidae and lives in meadows and hillsides where its foodplant, cowslip, grows. Sometimes it is found in woodland. It flies during May and June and hibernates in the pupal stage. The Duke of Burgundy Fritillary is not very common but not scarce. It has a wingspan of approximately 2 cm (1 in).

The Common Blue (*Polyommatus icarus*), a member of the Lycaenidae, is an extremely common and pretty butterfly found from May to September throughout Europe. Its favourite habitats are chalk downs, grassy hillsides, mountains and meadows. The female is brown, marked with blue and orange. Foodplants of the larvae are clovers and trefoils. Its wingspan is about 2 cm (1 in).

The Chalkhill Blue (*Lysandra corydon*), family Lycaenidae, is another species which is found extremely abundantly in certain localities. It favours chalk hills and grassy hillsides where its foodplant, horseshoe vetch, grows. The female is brown, but the markings are subject to tremendous variation. It hibernates in the egg stage. The wingspan is 2 cm (1 in).

The Holly Blue (*Celastrina argiolus*) is a delicate and attractive species of the Lycaenidae which occurs right across Eurasia to Japan. It is found in gardens, woods and shrubberies. The larvae feed on holly in spring but the autumn brood feeds on ivy; though both will accept other plants in captivity. It hibernates as a pupa. It has a wingspan of about 2 cm (1 in).

Chalkhill Blue

Small Copper

Holly Blue

Fiery Copper

The Small Copper (*Lycaena phlaeas*) is a very widespread and common lycaenid, occurring throughout Europe and across Asia to Japan. This little butterfly is found on rough ground, downs, heaths, open fields, banks and lanes. Small Coppers hibernate in the larval stage and produce more than one brood. The foodplant of the caterpillar is sheep's sorrel and occasionally common sorrel. The wingspan of the adult is about 2·5 cm (1 in).

The Fiery Copper (*Heodes virgaureae*), family Lycaenidae, is one of the 'large coppers' which is commonest in central Europe and is not found in Britain. The Fiery Copper inhabits meadows, edges of woodland and hillsides. The female is spotted with black and is less iridescent than the male. The larva feeds on docks. The wingspan is rather more than 2·5 cm (1 in).

Green Hairstreak

Purple Hairstreak

Brimstone

Clouded Yellow

The Green Hairstreak (*Callophrys rubi*) is a very widespread lycaenid and is common in certain localities. It is found right across Eurasia to Japan. It inhabits woodland clearings and edges, rough ground with bushes and chalk downs. Only the underside is green, the top side being dull brown. Food-plants are mainly trefoils, gorse, broom and allied plants, but dogwood and many others as well. The wingspan is less than 2·5 cm (1 in).

The Purple Hairstreak (*Thecla quercus*), family Lycaenidae, occurs in central and southern Europe, including Britain. It is found in oak woods, and is not rare but not one of the commoner species. The male is purple all over, but the female has purple only on the fore wings. The larva feeds on oak and hibernates. The wingspan is over 2·5 cm (1 in).

Clouded Yellows (*Colias crocea*), family Pieridae, are strong migrants. They are extremely common in parts of central Europe in lucerne fields, and over rough land and in meadows. They are commonest in Britain near the south coast. They breed on clover and lucerne, mainly in the Mediterranean countries. Larvae do not survive the winter in Britain. The wingspan is nearly 5 cm (2 in).

The Brimstone (*Gonepteryx rhamni*), family Pieridae, is found throughout northern Europe and across to Japan. It is common in the south of England, sometimes in gardens but it generally lives in or near woodland. The female is a pale greenish white. The larvae feed on buckthorn, sitting well camouflaged on the top surface of the leaves. Its wingspan is around 5 cm (2 in).

Orange Tips (*Anthocharis cardamines*) are common pierids in most parts of Eurasia to Japan. It is a wayside and hedge-row species, found also in damp meadows and in gardens. The female has no orange tips. The larvae are cannibalistic but feed principally on garlic mustard, cuckoo flower and other crucifers. Its wingspan is 3 cm (1 in).

The Wood White (*Leptidea sinapis*) is a pierid and has a very weak flight. It lives in woodland rides and clearings and is commonest in central Europe; it is not common in Britain. The female has paler wingtips. The larvae feed mainly on bitter vetch but will take other vetches and trefoils. The wingspan is a little over 2·5 cm (1 in).

Orange Tip   Wood White

The Apollo Butterfly (*Parnassius apollo*), family Papilionidae, is not found in Britain. This large species occurs mainly in mountainous parts of central and northern Europe, including Scandinavia. Some females are very transparent; and the markings vary considerably. After mating the female produces a prominent pouch from the underside of the abdomen which remains and prevents mating again. The wingspan is around 9 cm ($3\frac{1}{2}$ in).

The Swallowtail (*Papilio machaon*) is a papilionid found throughout Europe and northern Asia in many races and sub-species. It is mostly fairly common, but in England it is confined to parts of Norfolk. Larvae are magnificently striped in black and orange on green. Foodplants are milk parsley, wild carrot and other umbellifers. Its wingspan is up to 9 cm ($3\frac{1}{2}$ in).

The Scarce Swallowtail (*Iphiclides podalirius*), family Papilionidae, is found in some parts of northern Europe (not in Britain), but in southern Europe, and in Spain in particular, it is quite common. This species extends into north Africa. The larvae feed on blackthorn. The wingspan is around 7 to 9 cm (3 to $3\frac{1}{2}$ in).

Zerynthia polyxena is a small species of the Papilionidae which occurs in southern Europe from Portugal along the

Mediterranean to Persia. Most members of the genus *Zerynthia* have similar colouring and pattern; they all feed on species of *Aristolochia* (Dutchman's Pipe). *Zerynthia polyxena* flies in open fields, meadows and gardens. It has a wingspan of nearly 5 cm (2 in).

The Large Skipper (*Ochlodes venata*), family Hesperiidae, is a common species found throughout Europe and northern Asia, but hardly at all in Ireland and Scotland. It likes the edges of woodland, rough grassland, grassy hillsides and cliffs. It rests in typical skipper resting position and flies like a moth. Larvae feed on grasses. The wingspan is over 2·5 cm (1 in).

Dingy Skippers (*Erynnis tages*) are hesperids that are fond of open spaces, edges of woodland, heaths and grassy hills. They are common almost throughout Europe. At rest the wings are held flat over the body like a moth. The colour and flight also remind one of a moth. The larvae feed on bird's-foot trefoil. The wingspan is under 2·5 cm (1 in).

1 Apollo Butterfly
2 Swallowtail
3 Scarce Swallowtail
4 *Zerynthia polyxena*
5 Dingy Skipper
6 Large Skipper

North America

In this area are considered the species which occur in the north of Mexico, the United States, Canada and Alaska. This area, while having species very closely allied to those in other regions, tends to have its own species with overlap only occurring in the south. This is undoubtedly because of the barrier of ocean on all sides but the junction with South America. Here, in Mexico, it is possible to encounter certain of the South American genera such as *Megalura, Mechanitis, Callicore,* etc.

North America is rich in its population of fritillaries and has a number of Arctic species. Included in the 'fritillaries' are the numerous *Phyciodes, Boloria, Melitaea* and *Argynnis.* The commas or angle-wings (*Polygonia* species) have many representatives here also. There are interesting Arctic Satyridae, and *Colias* species are well represented, with fine Arctic species as well. *Parnassius* and *Papilio* species are widely distributed, there are about twenty-seven *Papilio* species in this region. There are several species of orange tips, *Catopsilia, Eurema* and *Dismorphia.* The theclas and hesperiids are numerous in North America.

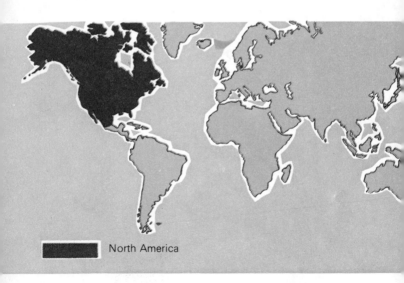

North America

Oenis gigas, family Satyridae, is a large species reminiscent of the Grayling, which occurs in Arctic America and Vancouver Island. It hides amongst dark mosses and fallen trees, the males darting out if disturbed or curious to investigate a passing insect. The larvae feed on grasses. It has a wingspan of nearly 7 cm ($2\frac{1}{2}$ in).

The Common Wood-nymph (*Satyrus alope*) is a satyrid that is fairly common throughout the North American continent with several named geographical forms. The eye-spot markings are not constant and in some forms they are almost completely absent. The larvae feed on grasses. Its wingspan is from 4 to 7 cm ($1\frac{1}{2}$ to $2\frac{1}{2}$ in).

The Monarch or Milkweed (*Danaus plexippus*) is an extraordinarily large species of the Danaidae, sometimes measuring 10 cm (4 in) or more. It is famous for its migratory flights right across the continent and indeed across the Atlantic to Europe. Gatherings before migration sometimes amount to thousands all hanging on nearby trees. The larvae are strongly marked with yellow and black rings; their foodplant is the milkweed.

1 *Oenis gigas*
2 Common Wood Nymph
3 Monarch or Milkweed

1 Viceroy
2 underside of Viceroy
3 *Aglais milberti*
4 Question Mark

Viceroys (*Limenitis archippus*) are curious nymphalids which distinctly mimic the colouring and pattern of Monarchs. very closely, though they are quite a lot smaller. They range from southern Canada to the southern states, and are found in gardens and open spaces. They are widespread but not abundant. Their wingspan is about 7 to 8 cm (2½ to 3 in).

Aglais milberti, family Nymphalidae, is a very close relative of the common European Small Tortoiseshell (*A. urticae*). It is distributed from Virginia north to Nova Scotia and the western coast. The larvae are gregarious and feed on stinging nettles. The wingspan is rather under 5 cm (2 in).

The Question Mark (*Polygonia interrogationis*) is one of North America's commonest nymphalids and is closely related to the European Comma Butterfly. It occurs in fields, gardens and open spaces throughout the summer, hibernating in the butterfly stage. It is not found on the Pacific coast but otherwise it is widespread and is found far north into Canada. The wingspan is 5 cm (2 in).

Buckeyes (*Precis coenia*). family Nymphalidae, are found principally in the southern states where they are common and in some years extremely abundant. They are subject to some variation and might be confused with *P.lavinia* and *genoveva* but these do not fly in the same locality. The larvae feed on plantain and antirrhinum. The wingspan is 4 cm (1½ in).

The Gulf Fritillary (*Deione vanillae*) is principally a southern species of nymphalid and is fairly common in Texas, near woodland and in gardens. It is not a true fritillary but the bright silver spangles in the underside are reminiscent of fritillaries. Larvae feed on passion plant. The wingspan is 7 cm (2½ in).

Mourning Cloaks (*Nymphalis antiopa*), family Nymphalidae, are known in Britain as Camberwell Beauties. These migratory butterflies are widespread throughout the north of America and sometimes are very common indeed. They are attracted to sap exuding from trees and to fruit orchards in autumn. The larvae feed on willows, poplars, elm and birch. Their wingspan is about 8 cm (3 in).

1 Buckeye
2 Gulf Fritillary
3 Mourning Cloak

Boloria triclaris. family **Nymphalidae**, is a little Arctic fritillary; it is found commonly throughout the northern parts of the United States and Canada. It is also found on the higher summits of the Rocky Mountains. The female is rather lighter than the male and slightly transparent. The life history of *Boloria triclaris* is unknown. Its wingspan is about 4 cm (1½ in).

Argynnis diana is a really magnificent fritillary in which both sexes are very strikingly marked. The female is the only blue fritillary in the world. The male has a central black area with a broad orange, marginal band. It is now a

Brenthis triclaris

male *Argynnis diana*

Lycaena sonorensis

female *A. diana*

Colorado Hairstreak

rare species occurring occasionally in the south-eastern states. The wingspan is 10 cm (4 in).

Lycaena sonorensis, family Lycaenidae, is a very pretty little butterfly and is one of the blues. It is found in open spaces and grassland and quite abundantly at times. *Lycaena sonorensis* occurs mainly in California and northern Mexico. The wingspan is rather less than 2·5 cm (1 in). Its life history is unknown.

The Colorado Hairstreak (*Thecla crysalus*), family Lycaenidae, is one of North America's most beautiful hairstreaks. It has an attractive underside, marked with white lines on fawn, and the hind wings bear red eye-spots. It is found in woodland rather uncommonly in south-western states. The wingspan is about 2·5 cm (1 in).

In Great Purple Hairstreaks (*Thecla halesus*) the upperside colour is the most wonderful iridescent bottle-green and purple, which changes in intensity with the direction of the light. The Great Purple Hairstreak is another southern species which is very common in Central America but even in Georgia and the Gulf states it is not altogether scarce. The foodplant of the caterpillar is oak. The wingspan is over 2·5 cm (1 in).

Eurema nicippe, family Pieridae, is one of an exceedingly abundant group of species, especially in Asia. *Nicippe* is a common species in parts of the southern states but it is rare in the north. It is very variable in shades of orange and yellow. The larval foodplants are leguminous. The wingspan is nearly 5 cm (2 in).

Great Purple Hairstreak

Eurema nicippe

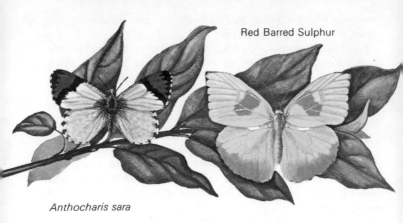

Red Barred Sulphur

Anthocharis sara

Anthocharis sara, family Pieridae, is a very pretty orange tip with the typical moss-green variegated pattern on the underside of the hind wings. It lives in the mountainous Pacific states of the USA. *Anthocharis sara* is not a very common species, but it is nevertheless subject to considerable variation and exists in a number of distinct forms known under different names. It has a wingspan of nearly 4 cm (1½ in).

The Red Barred Sulphur (*Catopsilia philea*) is a very fine pierid. It is primarily a South American species, being common in Brazil, Venezuela and Central America but its range extends north into Texas and occasionally as far as Illinois. The larvae feed on *Cassia* and may take other legumes. The wingspan is 8 cm (3 in) or more.

The Dog Face Butterfly (*Colias caesonia*), family Pieridae, has curious markings in yellow and black on the fore wings which very much resemble the profile of a poodle. The female is similar but paler in colour. This species is found right across the southern states. On the Pacific coast is found a close relative, *eurydice.* Its wingspan is about 7 cm (2½ in).

Tiger Swallowtails (*Papilio turnus*) are one of the world's finest papilionids. In the southern part of the range there is a curious, almost melanic form of the female (form *glaucus*) which is a pale chocolate colour all over. They are principally found in Pennsylvania, Ohio and Virginia. The larvae feed on wild cherry. Their wingspan is nearly 10 cm (4 in).

Dog Face Butterfly

Tiger Swallowtail

The Black Swallowtail (*Papilio asterias*) is a common swallowtail in the Atlantic states and south to the Mississippi, being found in gardens and open spaces. The larvae feed on many species of umbellifers and are often collected off carrots, parsley and fennel in gardens. This species will hybridize with the European *machaon*. Its wingspan is around 8 to 9 cm (3 to $3\frac{1}{2}$ in).

The Spice-bush Swallowtail (*Papilio troilus*), family Papilionidae, is commonly distributed throughout the southern Atlantic states. The caterpillar lives concealed, drawing the edges of the leaf together forming a hide. It feeds on spicewood and sassafras. The wingspan of the butterfly is around 9 cm ($3\frac{1}{2}$ in).

Parnassius smintheus, family Papilionidae, is one of two *Parnassius* species found in North America. It is subject

Black Swallowtail   Spice-bush Swallowtail

to tremendous variation and has many named forms. It is a mountain species found mainly in the Pacific states, from Colorado to California. The larvae feed on saxifrages and sedums. The wingspan is slightly over 5 cm (2 in).

Papilio ajax, family Papilionidae, is sometimes known as *marcellus*, which is the name given to its summer form. It has several named seasonal forms which are quite distinct. It ranges from the Appalachians to the foot of the Rocky Mountains, but is commonest in Kentucky and Indiana, in open spaces and gardens. The wingspan is about 8 cm (3 in).

The Long-tailed Skipper (*Eudamus proteus*) is an attractive hesperid, but is really a tropical species from Brazil and Central America and is related to the other long-tailed skippers from that region. This species is found along the Atlantic coast even as far north as New York, where it has been taken in Central Park. The larva feeds on wistaria. Its wingspan is nearly 5 cm (2 in).

1 *Parnassius smintheus*
2 *Papilio ajax*
3 Long-tailed Skipper

Central and South America

This region is easily defined, running south from Mexico to Cape Horn. South America has an abundance of butterflies that is unequalled by any other region in the world. The butterflies are unlike those found elsewhere: *Morpho, Heliconius, Ithomia, Agrias, Catagramma* and the tailed skippers all have no counterpart in the Old World. The magnificent owl butterflies (*Caligo*) also have no parallel. South American butterflies are unusually well endowed with brilliant reflective colours and iridescent shades which change according to the light and direction in which they are viewed. Superb examples of this are the *Ancyluris, Catagramma, Doxocopa, Agrias* species and of course the well known blue *Morpho* butterflies. The *Papilio* species in South America are numerous and the 'black papilios' in particular are very varied and often singularly attractive. Erycinids are at their strongest in this region and are represented by hundreds of species. Hesperiids are also very numerous and sometimes unusually attractive. In the south, the more temperate regions of Chile and Argentina are not so richly endowed but there are some very interesting local forms and species.

Central and South America

Pierella dracontis, family Satyridae, is one of a group of peculiarly shaped butterflies, some with lovely scarlet hindwings. It is a quite common Brazilian species. The wingspan is about 7 cm ($2\frac{1}{2}$ in).

Callitaera aurorina is a delicate satyrid from Colombia and the Amazon. It has almost transparent wings and a rose pink flush. It is fairly common. Its wingspan is about 7 cm ($2\frac{1}{2}$ in).

The species of the genus *Lycorea,* family Danaidae, are very similarly marked to the species of *Mechanitis* and *Heliconius.* They are weak fliers and frequent open places. *Lycorea cleobaea* is found in northern South America.

Ituna phenarete is a common ithiomiid found in Peru and Bolivia. It is a curious species with transparent wings. Its habits and life history are said to be similar to those of *Lycorea.* Its wingspan is 9 cm ($3\frac{1}{2}$ in).

Heliconius amaryllis, one of the huge heliconiid family, is common in northern Brazil and Peru. The larvae feed on passion plant. Its wingspan is about 8 cm (3 in).

Heliconius doris, family Heliconiidae, is distributed throughout the northern part of South America. This species is extremely common at all times. It is exceptionally variable; some specimens being marked with red or green.

Myscelia orsis, family Nymphalidae, has an intense blue colouring. It is a lovely species, and is not uncommon in parts of Brazil. The wingspan is approximately 4 cm ($1\frac{1}{2}$ in).

Ageronia velutina is a blue nymphalid with a brilliant splash of red on the underside. It makes a curious clicking sound when it moves its wings. It is common in Brazil. Its wingspan is about 7 cm ($2\frac{1}{2}$ in).

Agrias sardanapalus, family Nymphalidae, has various named forms and is one of the most beautiful of these gorgeous *Agrias.* It is one of the less rare ones and is found in the Amazon region. Its wingspan is about 9 cm ($3\frac{1}{2}$ in).

The nymphalid *Catagramma cynosura* is attractively marked on the underside and has brilliant upperside markings. It is common in Peru and Brazil. It has a wingspan of 5 cm (2 in).

The underside of *Catagramma excelsior* is almost identical to that of *cynosura.* Above, it is black, shot with royal blue, and marked in orange. It is common in Peru and Brazil.

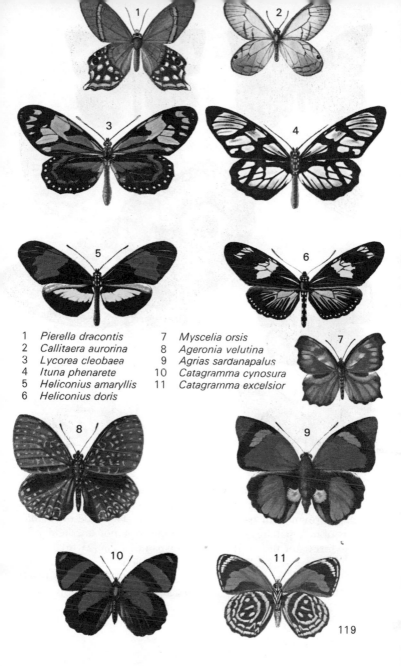

1 *Pierella dracontis*
2 *Callitaera aurorina*
3 *Lycorea cleobaea*
4 *Ituna phenarete*
5 *Heliconius amaryllis*
6 *Heliconius doris*
7 *Myscelia orsis*
8 *Ageronia velutina*
9 *Agrias sardanapalus*
10 *Catagramma cynosura*
11 *Catagramma excelsior*

Nessaea is a small nymphalid genus characterized by an unusual and bright, matt green underside. The upperside is dark brown with bars of clear sky-blue. The male of *obrinus* has orange patches on the hind wing. It is not uncommon in the forests of Brazil. It has a wingspan of 7 cm (2½ in).

The genus *Callicore* is closely allied to *Catagramma*. *Callicore* undersides are invariably silvery grey with black patterning in the form of circles and figures; the uppersides are often quite dissimilar. *Callicore neglecta* is common in

Morpho aega

Morpho achilles

1	female *Nessaea obrinus*	5	Owl Butterfly
2	male *N. obrinus*	6	male *Callithea sapphira*
3	underside of *N. obrinus*	7	female *C. sapphira*
4	*Callicore neglecta*	8	underside of *C. sapphira*

Brazil and Peru. Its wingspan is 4 cm ($1\frac{1}{2}$ in).

Callithea sapphira, family Nymphalidae, has males and females that are totally different. The male has the most exquisite blue iridescence, varying in intensity, on a black ground colour. It is an exceedingly local species found in the Amazon forest, in just a few places where the butterflies congregate to drink. Its wingspan is around 5 cm (2 in).

The Owl Butterfly (*Caligo atreus*) is a magnificent species of the Brassolidae and is probably the largest of the caligos, reaching well over 15 cm (6 in) across. The characteristic 'owl' markings are distinct and bright and the upperside has bands of bright purple and orange. Most *Caligo* species are not as bright on the upperside. The larvae feed on banana.

Morpho aega is one of the smallest of the Morphidae and the male is one of the brightest. The males occur in a ratio of about 1000 to 1 female. It is common, but in a restricted range at the extreme south of Brazil. The females are generally yellow ochre but there are blue forms and others which are mixed. The wingspan is 8 to 9 cm (3 to $3\frac{1}{2}$ in).

Morpho achilles is a magnificent and quite large species of *Morpho*. It is about 15 cm (6 in) across with a striking underside marked with lines and circles of green, yellow and red. The upperside band of blue varies in width and shape of colour according to the geographic region. *Achilles* occurs throughout tropical America.

Ancyluris formosissima

Morpho hecuba

Morpho rhetenor

Lyropteryx apollonia

Helicopis acis

Morpho didius

122

Morpho hecuba is the largest *Morpho* of all, reaching 20 to 25 cm (8 to 10 in) across. The wings are never iridescent blue but there is a lavender blue form (*cisseis*) which occurs in the Lower Amazon. This species occurs throughout the Amazon region and has many forms. It has a strong flight and travels for many miles.

The male of *Morpho rhetenor* is certainly one of the brightest of the Morphidae. It is subject to variation and has a form with a broad transverse white band (*pseudocypris*). The female has more rounded wings and is larger. It is always yellow ochre. *Rhetenor* occurs in the forests of northern Brazil and Guyana. Its wingspan is 12 to 15 cm (5 to 6 in).

Morpho didius is the largest of the all-blue species of *Morpho*. The female is brown, banded with blue, and is not unlike the female of *M.menelaus*. *Didius* comes mainly from Peru where, in the forest regions, it is abundant. Its wingspan is 15 to 17 cm (6 to 7 in).

Ancyluris formosissima, family Erycinidae, is one of the loveliest butterflies in the world. This small, beautifully shaped butterfly has equally bright colouring on each side of the wings. Not only does the blue change with the direction of the light but so too does the underside red band. It is rare and is chiefly found in Peru. It has a wingspan of 4 cm (1$\frac{1}{2}$ in).

Lyropteryx apollonia is an uncommon species found in Brazil, Peru and Ecuador. It lives in tropical forest clearings and along river banks. Like the other Erycinidae it is small, about 4 cm (1$\frac{1}{2}$ in) across, but extremely colourful. The green-rayed pattern is unusual in butterflies and the underside spotting in pink is a lovely contrast with this dark green.

Helicopis acis, family Erycinidae, is the largest species in this genus which has an unusual and characteristic wing shape with multi-tails. The markings, cream and orange on brown, are common to nearly all *Helicopis*. *Acis* in particular has the most delightful raised silver spangles on the underside. It is found in Brazil. The wingspan is around 5 cm (2 in).

Thecla coronata, family Lycaenidae, must be the world's most beautiful hairstreak. The underside is illustrated; above it is deep royal blue all over. It is from Ecuador and Colombia. The wingspan is over 5 cm (2 in).

Catopsilia avellaneda, family Pieridae, is a rare species, restricted to Cuba, and much sought by collectors. The female is even redder than the male. Its wingspan is 10 cm (4 in).

The pierid *Gonepteryx menippe* is a giant relative of the European brimstones. It is common throughout tropical America, even at high altitudes. Its wingspan is up to 10 cm (4 in).

Dismorphia are peculiarly shaped pierid butterflies. This genus is related to the European Wood White. *D.orise* lives in forest clearings and likes to bask in the sun. It is common in Brazil. The wingspan is 5 to 7 cm (2 to $2\frac{1}{2}$ in).

For a pierid the colouring of *Pereute callinice* is unusual and resembles the heliconiids. This species is common in Peru. It has a wingspan of 5 to 7 cm (2 to $2\frac{1}{2}$ in).

The male of *Perrhybris lorena* is a typical black and white pierid but the female is quite different and mimics *Mechanitis*. It is common in Peru and Colombia. Its wingspan is 7 cm ($2\frac{1}{2}$ in).

Papilio protesilaus, family Papilionidae, belongs to a group of species which are all remarkably similar. *Protesilaus* is very common and sometimes found feeding from damp patches in hundreds. Its wingspan is 8 cm (3 in).

Papilio thoas is a large swallowtail, nearly 15 cm (6 in) across. It is common throughout Brazil and Peru and is fond of forest clearings and orchards. The larvae feed on *Citrus*.

Papilio childrenae is one of the most beautiful of the 'black papilios' but rather scarce. The green of the fore wing is a lovely clear, shining colour. It is found in Central America and Colombia. The wingspan is 8 cm (3 in).

Papilio thyastes is a rarer species, and is the most beautiful of the sword-tailed swallowtails. It is found in forest clearings in Brazil, Peru and Bolivia. Its wingspan is 8 cm (3 in).

The hesperiid *Erycides zonara* is over four times the size of the related European skippers. It is common in Brazil and has a wingspan of nearly 7 cm ($2\frac{1}{2}$ in).

1	*Thecla coronata*	7	*Papilio protesilaus*
2	*Catopsilia avellaneda*	8	*Papilio thoas*
3	*Gonepteryx menippe*	9	*Papilio childrenae*
4	*Dismorphia orise*	10	*Papilio thyastes*
5	*Pereute callinice*	11	*Erycides zonara*
6	*Perrhybis lorena*		

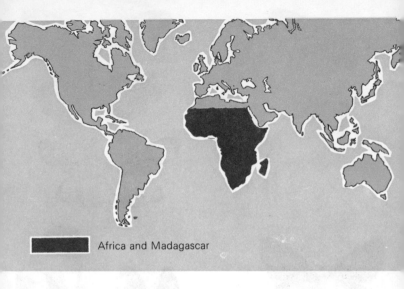

Africa and Madagascar

In this region species found south of the Sahara and south of the Red Sea are being considered. Africa does not have as many beautiful species as South America and the total number of species is considerably fewer. Nevertheless there are many interesting species and local forms in the different geographical areas.

Africa is the stronghold of the *Charaxes* and there are many species distributed throughout the entire region. Papilios are not numerous but some are extremely attractive. Two are very spectacular: *Papilio antimachus* and *Papilio zalmoxis* which are comparable in size with the birdwings of New Guinea. There are a great many Pieridae, some rather dull, but some, notably the *Colotis*, are amongst the most beautiful in the world. There are more *Colotis* here than elsewhere in the world. *Acraea* species, too, are most numerous in Africa. These are often mimicked and this phenomenon occurs with other species very conspicuously in Africa. There are numbers of mostly small Nymphalidae, many of which are only found in Africa. The Lycaenidae are numerous and there are some fine coppers.

Table Mountain Beauty

Trimen's Brown

Amauris niavius

The Table Mountain Beauty (*Aeropetes tulbaghia*) is a magnificent satyrid which occurs from Cape Town north to Rhodesia. It is a mountain species, not often common, though widely spread. Sometimes it is attracted to gardens and apparently favours red flowers. The flight season of this species starts in December and goes on till May. Its wingspan is 8 cm (3 in).

Trimen's Brown, *Melampias trimenii,* is a South African satyrid which might be compared with the European species of *Erebia* in its flight and habits. It is a grass feeder which inhabits mountains, but is rarely found in great numbers. It is one of a group with similar colouring. The wingspan is about 4 cm ($1\frac{1}{2}$ in).

Amauris niavius, family Danaidae, is primarily a forest species. This butterfly is found throughout the year from South Africa right up to equatorial Africa. In parts it is scarce, but not everywhere. It is mimicked by *Papilio dardanus* and several nymphalids. It has a strong acrid smell. The wingspan is about 9 cm ($3\frac{1}{2}$ in).

Limnas alcippus

Acraea egina (male)

A. egina (female)

Acraea anemosa

Limnas alcippus, family Danaidae, is a geographical form of *Limnas chrysippus* which is widespread and common throughout Africa and Asia. *Limnas alcippus* is found in equatorial regions and, more rarely, further south. It is mimicked by a form of *Hypolimnas misippus*. The larvae feed on various plants of the genus *Asclepias*. It has a wingspan of 5 to 7 cm (2 to $2\frac{1}{2}$ in).

Acraea egina, family Acraeidae, is a particularly colourful species. It is common in parts of west Africa but much less known in the east. It is mimicked by *Papilio ridleyanus* and curiously both these species have a similar red colour which fades quickly. The female of *egina* is a dull orange colour. Its wingspan is around 5 cm (2 in).

Acraea anemosa, family Acraeidae, is one of the most beautiful of the *Acraea* species found in the south. It is mostly found in Natal and is never very common. It has a slow, rather weak flight, stopping to feed at flowers high up in thorn trees. Only occasionally does it come to the ground. The wingspan is 4 cm ($1\frac{1}{2}$ in).

Crenis rosa, family Nymphalidae, is a small butterfly with particularly unusual colouring. It is found only in central Africa; it occurs mainly in Zambia and Rhodesia. The underside is bright orange with black dots and markings set in areas of silvery grey. It lives in forest regions. It has a wingspan of nearly 5 cm (2 in).

Cymothoe sangaris is an equatorial species of nymphalid and one of the loveliest in the world. No other butterfly surpasses its deep blood red colour. *Cymothoe sangaris* is a small butterfly, but other somewhat similar species occur in the same region. It is widely distributed in equatorial forest, in clearings and along paths. The wingspan is under 5 cm (2 in).

Precis octavia, family Nymphalidae, has two very distinctly different forms in the summer and winter. Until comparatively recently the two forms were considered to be different species. The pink form emerges in September (spring in the southern hemisphere) and the blue form is produced in March. It is mainly found in southern Africa. It has a wingspan of 5 cm (2 in).

Crenis rosa

Cymothoe sangaris

Precis octavia sesamus

Precis octavia

male

female

Hypolimnas misippus

Hypolimnas misippus is a nymphalid that occurs throughout Africa and Asia. The male colouring is constant, but the female varies from one region to another according to the butterfly which it mimics. Its model is usually one of the forms of *Limnas chrysippus*. It has a swift flight; and occurs in gardens and open spaces. The wingspan is 7 cm ($2\frac{1}{2}$ in).

Salamis species are lovely mother of pearl nymphalid butterflies. They are only found in Africa. *S. parhassus* occurs from Natal right up to the equatorial forests. It likes forest clearings, streams and paths best but is also attracted to gardens. It generally flies high and is difficult to catch. Its wingspan is 8 cm (3 in) or more.

Charaxes bohemani is a very handsome species of nymphalid. The blue colouring is rather unusual in *Charaxes*. It is found chiefly in Zambia and Rhodesia but extends further north and, occasionally goes south, into South Africa. It is a powerful flier, which keeps to the tree tops, but it can be lured down to bait. The wingspan is 8 to 9 cm (3 to $3\frac{1}{2}$ in).

Charaxes jasius saturnus is another very fine nymphalid which is seldom common. But it is sometimes found in small groups taking nourishment from damp patches, sap, dead animals, etc. It is chiefly found in Zambia and Rhodesia but extends south into South Africa. The underside is particularly beautiful. It has a wingspan of 8 cm (3 in).

Spindasis natalensis is a common lycaenid which occurs throughout the southern part of Africa. It is a woodland species, but is occasionally attracted into gardens. It sits

Salamis parhassus

Charaxes bohemani

head downwards, moving its hind wings up and down so that its tails wave about like antennae. The wings have lovely silver-streaked undersides. Its wingspan is 2·5 cm (1 in).

Aphnaeus hutchinsoni, family Lycaenidae, is a hairstreak that is very rare and restricted to small areas of southern Africa. It frequents hot, dry, open spaces where it breeds amongst gnarled thorn trees, the larvae burrowing into the wood. The larvae also feed on mistletoe. The male is smaller than the female. It has a wingspan around 2·5 cm (1 in).

Charaxes jasius saturnus

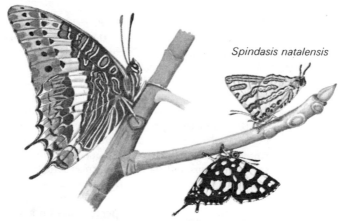

Spindasis natalensis

Aphnaeus hutchinsoni

Colotis erone (left)
Colotis euippe (upper right)
Eronia cleodora (lower right)

Colotis erone is a coastal species of the Pieridae found in the region of Durban. Only the male has the lovely iridescent purple tip to the fore wings. The female more resembles a Cabbage White and has only black tips to the wings. It is generally common, particularly in the south. The species flies throughout the year but is less active from June to September. It has a wingspan of about 5 cm (2 in). It is one of a large family of butterflies with coloured tips, ranging from yellows and oranges, through reds to purples and blues.

Colotis euippe, family Pieridae, is a very variable species with both seasonal forms and natural variation which make it difficult to identify. The amount of black on all wings, and the central black bar, in particular, varies tremendously so that it is easily confused with allied species. It occurs almost throughout the African continent, at all times of the year. It prefers woodland or shrubby places and avoids open grassland. It has a wingspan of a little over 2·5 cm (1 in).

Eronia cleodora is a species of pierid which is particularly common in the extreme south around Durban. It is also found further north, but, curiously, although so common in southern parts, it is prized by northern collectors as a rarity. It does not fly high and keeps to the edge of forest. From June to October it is much scarcer. It has a wingspan of rather over 5 cm (2 in).

Papilio antimachus, family Papilionidae, is the largest butterfly on the African continent; the males may reach up to 25 cm (10 in) in wingspan. No other butterfly in the world has this curious long, narrow wing shape. The female is not so large and is paler in colouring. The first female was only discovered in 1915 by an expedition made for Lord Rothschild (though the male was known in 1785). Possibly fewer than six females have ever been collected and years go by without any being seen. Yet the males, in certain places, abound every year. The life history and foodplant of this mystery butterfly are completely unknown though considerable efforts have been made to investigate its habits. The body of *Papilio antimachus* contains enough poison to kill six cats and it is thought that the poison may be derived from the larval foodplant. The species is only found in the deepest forests of equatorial Africa and is considered as a great rarity.

Papilio antimachus

Papilio zalmoxis is a fine Papilionid butterfly. It is the second largest in Africa and is found in similar regions to *antimachus*. It is quite a lot more common but still a great find and is a considerable rarity. Like the previous species the females are virtually never seen. This species may have a wingspan of about 15 cm (6 in). Both *zalmoxis* and *antimachus* are comparable with the birdwings found in New Guinea and East Indian islands but nowhere else can these magnificent giants be found.

Papilio dardanus is a truly remarkable Papilionid butterfly. The female forms differ from the male and from each other. Some forms are black with large patches of white. Others are marked with shades of brown and some are almost completely brown so that none are easily recognisable as the same species. Such extreme natural variation does not occur in any other species in the world. In Madagascar the female resembles the male, being cream and black with tails. The different forms mimic the distasteful Danaidae and are not tailed like the male. It is found throughout Africa.

Papilio nireus is a common and very beautiful swallowtail found throughout Africa. It is a woodland species primarily, but is attracted to gardens and orchards. The larvae feed on *Citrus*. Southern examples have a narrower blue band. It has a wingspan of about 7 cm (3 in).

Papilio demodocus, family Papilionidae, is probably Africa's best known butterfly and it is found in all regions. It flies at all times of the year but is commonest in December in the south.

The larvae feed on citrus trees and can cause damage in orchards. It is seldom seen in quantity but is always around. It has a wingspan of about 8 cm (3 in).

Acleros mackenii, family Hesperiidae, is quite a common little butterfly in South Africa where it is found at the edges of woodland and in clearings. It prefers shady places, skipping from flower to flower. It flies throughout the year and is sometimes as common in winter as it is in summer. It has a wingspan of less than 2·5 cm (1 in).

1   *Papilio zalmoxis*
2   *Papilio dardanus*
3   *Papilio nireus*
4   *Papilio demodocus*
5   *Acleros mackenii* (underside)

Australia, New Guinea and New Zealand

This region has a very interesting selection of butterflies ranging from the temperate species in the south, across desert to the tropical beauties occurring in northern Australia and New Guinea. Across the region as a whole, there is a good representation of the main butterfly families, consisting of more than 500 species.

Australia has a rather different terrain and vegetation from that found on other continents and consequently produces species and geographical forms not found elsewhere. Tropical New Guinea even today has not been completely explored and almost certainly there are mountain species which have yet to be discovered. Some of these mountains are high and very inaccessible; they are also inhabited by head-hunting natives. On the Australian mainland butterflies are most numerous in the coastal rain forests, and especially so in Queensland. Interesting species are found nevertheless on the open grasslands, heaths and in the Australian Alps in Victoria. New Zealand has very few species indeed and some of those which are there today are migrants which have established themselves in recent years.

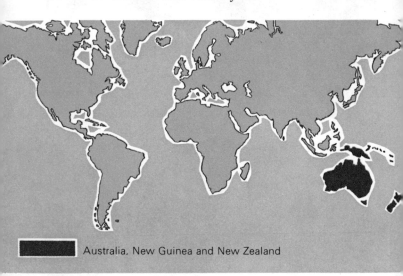

Australia, New Guinea and New Zealand

Heteronympha merope

Danaus melissa

Euploea callithae hansemanni

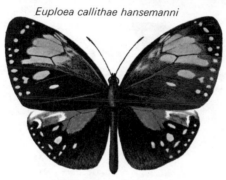

Heteronympha, family Satyridae, is a genus that is found only in Australia but is very reminiscent of the European Wall Brown (*Pararge megera*). *H.merope* occurs in the south and is common in woodlands and mountain slopes. Males appear weeks before the females emerge. It has a wingspan of 5 to 7 cm (2 to 2½ in).

Euploea callithae hansemanni, family Danaidae, is a magnificent but rather scarce species which occurs over most of New Guinea and on some of the nearby islands. It is one of the largest of the 'crow butterflies' and occurs in at least ten different geographical forms. It has a very characteristic slow, flapping flight. The wingspan is around 11 cm (4½ in).

Danaus melissa is very widely distributed right across Asia. This danaid also occurs in New Guinea and its neighbouring islands, and south across Australia to New South Wales. There are many forms – the Australian form is *hamata*. It is a woodland species which likes shady places. It has a wingspan of around 8 cm (3 in).

Cethosia chrysippe

Polyura pyrrhus

Vanessa gonerilla

Taenaris catops

Cethosia chrysippe, family Nymphalidae, is a very beautiful 'lacewing butterfly' with an intricately patterned underside. It occurs throughout the tropical islands to the north of Australia and also in Queensland. It is not found in quantity, but is not a rarity. The larvae feed on *Passiflora* and are gregarious. The wingspan is about 8 cm (3 in).

Polyura pyrrhus, is a nymphalid that is closely allied to the genus *Charaxes*. This butterfly has a powerful flight and occurs in forest areas, flying high out of reach. It is attracted to fermenting fruit and dung. It occurs in the tropical regions but also ranges further south into New South Wales. Its wingspan is about 8 cm (3 in).

Vanessa gonerilla, family Nymphalidae, is a close relative of the Red Admiral and Painted Lady. It is found only in New Zealand where it is not uncommon. The larvae feed on stinging nettles. On Chatham Island, 500 miles away to the east, there is a different form known as *Vanessa gonerilla ida*. The wingspan is a little less than 5 cm (2 in).

The species of *Taenaris* form a peculiar group of

butterflies in the family Amathusiidae. They have huge ringed eye-spots on a pale background. They are immensely variable and occur in New Guinea and nearby islands. *Taenaris catops* is a common species which frequents the edges of forests and is often seen flying at dusk. It has a wingspan of 8 to 9 cm (3 to $3\frac{1}{2}$ in).

Libythea geoffroyi

Libythea geoffroyi is the most beautiful of all the libytheids in the world. It is very rare in Australia, and is seen only in the extreme north of the Cape York Peninsula and in the Northern Territory near to Darwin. In parts of New Guinea it is commoner. The larvae feed on nettle. The palps are extended curiously giving the appearance of a beak. It has a wingspan of nearly 5 cm (2 in).

Ialmenus evagoras

Ialmenus evagoras, family Lycaenidae, is a rather common but lovely hairstreak which occurs right across Australia. There are three forms, the tropical one being nearly continuously brooded. The larvae are gregarious and feed on *Acacia* species, usually attended by ants which take a sweet secretion produced by the larvae. It has a wingspan of just over 2·5 cm (1 in).

Thysonotis danis serapis

Liphyra brassolis major

Thysonotis danis serapis is a gorgeous, tropical lycaenid which flies deep in jungle recesses and clearings. It occurs in the northern part of the Cape York Peninsula and throughout the lower altitudes of New Guinea. Basically it is a common species but its habitats are unfortunately often rather inaccessible. The wings have a lovely metallic colouring. Its wingspan is 4 cm (1½ in).

Liphyra brassolis major is the largest lycaenid found in Australia. Its larvae live in the nests of green tree ants, feeding on ant larvae. The pupa is formed within the hard protective larval skin and, on emergence, the butterfly is covered with loose white scales which stick to any ants which attack it. Unlike other lycaenids, it is an enemy of ants. This species is only found in Queensland.

Delias harpalyce, family Pieridae, is a very beautiful southern species occurring mainly on low land but sometimes also in mountains. The top side is not brightly coloured as with the other species of *Delias*. The larvae live and, curiously, pupate gregariously. They feed on mistletoe. They are common in some years but are never abundant. Their wingspan is 7 cm (2½ in).

Delias mysis is a tropical pierid, occurring in New Guinea and in Australia from Queensland across to Darwin. It is not a common species but it is found sometimes in groups. The larvae and pupae, like *harpalyce*, are gregarious and feed on mistletoe. The butterfly is fond of visiting lantana flowers. Its wingspan is around 5 cm (2 in).

Delias aruna has a number of very different named forms with completely different colouring. *Delias aruna inferna* is perhaps the best known and occurs in New Guinea and the Cape York Peninsula. The other forms are found in New Guinea only. One form with large red patches is found in the western part of the island. The wingspan is nearly 8 cm (3 in).

Papilio weiskei, family Papilionidae, is a very unusual butterfly which is only found in the mountains of New Guinea. It is considered a great rarity, though in the places where it is seen there are usually quantities of the butterflies, clustering at damp patches or flying about the forest. The lilac colour is unique. Its wingspan is 6 cm (2½ in).

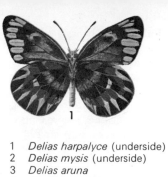

1 *Delias harpalyce* (underside)
2 *Delias mysis* (underside)
3 *Delias aruna*
4 *Papilio weiskei*
5 *Papilio ulysses*
6 *Ornithoptera paradisea*
7 *Cressida cressida*

Cressida cressida is a strange papilionid. It bears a striking resemblance to the *Parnassius* species, although these are not found in Australia. The females produce a similar pouch after mating. The wings are very transparent (especially in the female). It is a tropical species occurring in northern Australia and southern New Guinea. The wingspan is about 8 cm (3 in).

Papilio ulysses, family Papilionidae, is one of the handsomest butterflies in the world. This large swallowtail is about 12 cm (5 in) across. It has very many forms according to its locality. It is found in New Guinea, the Solomon Isles and neighbouring islands and in Queensland too. The brightest form is called *joesa*. It is commoner in the wet season.

Ornithoptera paradisea, family Papilionidae, is one of the birdwings. They are the most prized butterflies in the world, and this with its elegantly curved tails and shimmering gold and green colouring must be one of the loveliest. It flies in New Guinea both in the mountains and on parts of the coast. It is very scarce and is seldom found. The male is about 15 cm (6 in) across, the female is about 20 cm (8 in).

Ornithoptera alexandrae is another birdwing. The female of this species is the largest of all butterflies, nearly 25 cm (10 in) across. Female *Ornithoptera* are shades of brown and unlike the male in shape. *Ornithoptera alexandrae* is very scarce and is only found in the lowland forests of central and northern New Guinea. The male is 17 to 20 cm (7 to 8 in) across.

Ornithoptera goliath is an extremely beautiful papilionid. Its colouring defies description and the shine is difficult to illustrate. It occurs all over New Guinea but is exceedingly rare in collections. Several different forms exist from various parts of the island. The males have a wingspan of 17 to 20 cm (7 to 8 in), females are 22 cm (9 in) across.

Ornithoptera priamus, family Papilionidae, is a birdwing that is not at all rare and is extremely widespread throughout New Guinea, northern parts of Australia and the adjoining islands. Very many geographical forms occur and the Australian (Queensland) form, *Ornithoptera priamus euphorion* is one of the loveliest. *Ornithoptera priamus poseidon*, the mainland New Guinea form, is the commonest. Males have a wingspan of around 12 to 17 cm (5 to 7 in).

Ornithoptera alexandrae

Ornithoptera goliath

Ornithoptera priamus

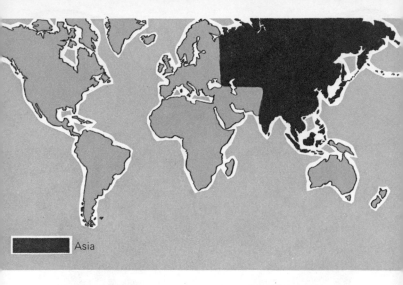

Asia

Asia

The area considered under this heading is very wide and takes in several rather different groups of butterfly fauna, but most of these groups have many species in common with others and there is a great deal of overlap. The area extends eastwards across India and Ceylon (Ceylon has a good many endemic species), Burma, China and Korea to Japan. To the south the region includes Thailand, the Malay peninsula, Borneo, the Philippines, Sumatra, Java and Celebes. The species in the last mentioned islands bear affinity to those found in New Guinea, while in a westerly direction, Borneo and Sumatra have butterflies which are more akin to those in Malaysia and Thailand. In Burma the species become more like the Indian and Chinese fauna.

There is no one particular part of Asia where there is an unusual abundance of butterflies as each part has its good regions. The northern hills of India are rich, the Malaysian Highlands, the Borneo rain forests and the isle of Taiwan (Formosa) all have many species in abundance. There are many interesting island forms to be found in the East Indies and probably still many more to be discovered.

Melanitis leda is a very large satyrid. It is one of the most widely distributed species in this region. It certainly extends beyond Asia and undoubtedly occurs in all parts of the continent. *Melanitis leda* is extremely variable in size, pattern and colouring. The larvae feed, often in colonies, on coarse grasses. The wingspan is 5 to 8 cm (2 to 3 in).

Melanitis leda

Elymnias hypermnestra, family Satyridae, is a common species in a genus of curious butterflies which are strongly mimetic and polymorphic. It is distributed throughout Asia. The male is sometimes mainly black and deep purple, or as illustrated, or even rayed with pale green. There are many other forms too. The larvae feed on palm. Its wingspan is 5 to 7 cm (2 to 2½ in).

Elymnias hypermnestra

Euploea mulciber, family Danaidae, is another very common and widespread butterfly found throughout Asia. The male is beautifully coloured with shining purple; the female, however, is less brightly coloured and has a streaked pattern. It is a forest species which likes clearings, paths and dried up water courses. It has a wingspan of around 8 cm (3 in).

Euploea mulciber

1 *Euploea diocletianus*
2 *Prothoe calydonia*
3 *Hestia leuconoe*

4 *Polyura delphis*
5 *Neptis* species
6 *Cyrestris thyodamas*

Euploea diocletianus is a less common danaid, restricted to Borneo, the Malay peninsula, and northern India. It has several geographical forms, but none is startlingly different. This species avoids damp places and is a frequent visitor to flowers. Its wingspan is less than 8 cm (3 in).

Prothoe calydonia is a nymphalid. The underside of this butterfly is exquisitely coloured. *Prothoe* is allied to *Charaxes* and will also come to bait. A powerful forest flier, *P.calydonia* is found only in Malaya and Borneo. It is very scarce indeed. The wingspan is about 9 cm ($3\frac{1}{2}$ in).

Hestia leuconoe is an impressive danaid butterfly with large papery wings which enable it to float on the air like a kite. It is very common in Formosa and the Philippines. Allied *Hestia* species are found in Malaysia and the East Indian islands. They are all woodland butterflies which like watery places. Their wingspan is about 15 cm (6 in).

Polyura delphis, a nymphalid, is most beautifully coloured on the underside but the upperside too is a lovely creamy white, marked with very pale blue. It occurs in the forests of Malaysia, Borneo and Sumatra, and is also found in India. The wingspan is over 8 cm (3 in).

Neptis is a genus of the Nymphalidae that is closely related to *Limenitis*. A particular species has not been singled out because there are nearly a hundred, mostly very alike, distributed throughout the region. They are woodland and forest species with a characteristic flipping movement in their flight. *Neptis* are also well represented in Africa by some thirty species. Their wingspan is about 4 cm ($1\frac{1}{2}$ in).

Cyrestris thyodamas is a fairly common and curiously marked nymphalid which is found in China, northern India, Formosa and some of the Pacific islands. There are many *Cyrestris* species which have been given the name 'map butterflies' because of their markings. They are mainly forest species and are fond of water. Their wingspan is around 5 cm (2 in).

Kaniska canace is a widely distributed vanessid which occurs in all parts of Asia. The blue colouring is not found in its European relatives. Its wingspan is nearly 5 cm (2 in).

Doleschallia bisaltidae, family Nymphalidae, is one of the 'leaf butterflies' rather resembling the American *Zaretes*. It is extremely variable and widespread throughout the region. There are many species in this genus. The wingspan is over 5 cm (2 in).

Kallima philarchus is a magnificent leaf butterfly. It is a native of Ceylon. It is not common and flies high, well out of reach. The wingspan is 10 cm (4 in).

Cethosia myrina, family Nymphalidae, is a very beautiful lacewing butterfly from Celebes. It only occurs in one small area and is not at all common. It has a sweet perfume which persists even when dead. It has a wingspan of 8 cm (3 in).

Stichopthalma camadeva, family Amathusiidae, is a very large, round-winged species which is found chiefly in the hills of northern India. It has a slow, flapping flight and is out at dawn and dusk. The wingspan is around 12 cm (5 in).

Thaumantis diores is a beautiful, *Morpho*-like amathusid from the hills of Assam. It flies only at sunset or afterwards and is attracted to rotting fruit. Its wingspan is around 10 cm (4 in).

Arhopala centaurus, family Lycaenidae, is one of a large group of royal blue hairstreaks which occur throughout Asia. All are shade loving forest species. Their wingspan is 4 cm (1½ in).

A particular species of *Jamides* has not been selected because there is a multitude found throughout Asia. These lycaenids are sometimes so common that grassland seems to be carpeted with them. They have a wingspan of 2·5 cm (1 in).

Neocheritra amrita is a Malayan hairstreak with very long, flowing tails. It is a tree-loving species which is not very common. The wingspan is 4 cm (1½ in).

Common grass yellows, of the family Pieridae, are found all over Asia. *Eurema hecabe* is one of the commonest. It has a low, fluttering flight. The wingspan is 2·5 cm (1 in).

Ixias pyrene, family Pieridae, is found all over Asia. This butterfly has numerous geographical forms, some of which

1 *Kaniska canace*
2 *Doleschallia bisaltidae*
3 *Kallima philarchus*
4 *Cethosia myrina*
5 *Stichopthalma camadeva*

6 *Arhopala centaurus*
7 *Jamides* species
8 *Thaumantis diores*
9 *Neocheritra amrita*
10 *Eurema hecabe*

are quite unlike the typical form. It is also subject to great seasonal variation. The wingspan is 2 to 5 cm (1 to 2 in).

Hebomoia vossi comes from two tiny islands, Nias and Batu, in the East Indies. It resembles the white *H. glaucippe*. It has a wingspan of 9 cm (3½ in).

Catopsilia scylla, family Pieridae, has a curious contrast of yellow hind wings and white fore wings. This coloration is not seen in any other species. It is fairly common in gardens and open ground in Java. It has a wingspan of 5 cm (2 in).

Delias hyparete, family Pieridae, is a very common species from India and South East Asia. It occurs in distinct geographical forms. It is gregarious and is sometimes seen in groups of fifty or more. The wingspan is 6 cm (2½ in).

Papilio sarpedon, family Papilionidae, is probably the commonest Asian swallowtail. It occurs in gardens, forests and open spaces in a number of brightly coloured geographical forms. It has a wingspan of 5 to 8 cm (2 to 3 in).

Papilio paris is a lovely species found principally in northern India but forms occur throughout China and into Formosa. Allied species occur in Borneo and Sumatra. Their wingspan is 7 to 10 cm (2½ to 4 in).

Papilio peranthus is rather a rare species of papilionid that is found mainly in Java. It frequents clearings in the rain forest and likes to fly over water. It is also fond of visiting *Lantana* flowers. It has a wingspan of 8 to 9 cm (3 to 3½ in).

Papilio blumei is one of the most magnificent papilios. This large swallowtail has a wingspan of 12 cm (5 in). It is only found in Celebes.

The combination of magenta and black on the underside of *Papilio horishanus* is unique. It is restricted to central Formosa. It has a wingspan of 10 to 12 cm (4 to 5 in).

The papilionid *Troides aeacus* is one of the commonest of a group of large black and yellow birdwings and comes from

1	*Ixias pyrene*	7	*Papilio paris*
2	*Hebomoia vossi*	8	*Papilio blumei*
3	*Catopsilia scylla*	9	*Papilio horishanus*
4	*Delias hyparete*	10	male *Troides aeacus*
5	*Papilio sarpedon*	11	female
0	*Papilio peranthus*		

China, India and the Malay peninsula. The larvae feed on *Aristolochia*. It has a wingspan of 10 to 17 cm (4 to 7 in).

Trogonoptera brookiana is a superb and graceful papilionid butterfly found chiefly in Malaya but in Borneo and Sumatra also. The males congregate in groups of twenty to fifty over damp ground. It is a forest species found mainly in the highlands. The female is very scarce. The wingspan is 15 to 17 cm (6 to 7 in).

Only two species in the Papilionidae have the peculiar wing shape of *Papilio coon*. It occurs in Malaya on the plains and lower hills and also in northern Java. The larvae are *Aristolochia* feeders. It has a wingspan of 8 to 10 cm (3 to 4 in).

Rhopalocampta benjamini, family Hesperiidae, is a giant skipper which is not uncommon throughout China and India and ranges south in Malaysia. This species likes open grassy spaces and the edges of forest, sometimes flying at night. Its wingspan is about 4 cm ($1\frac{1}{2}$ in).

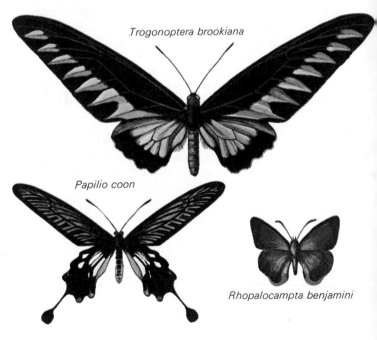

Trogonoptera brookiana

Papilio coon

Rhopalocampta benjamini

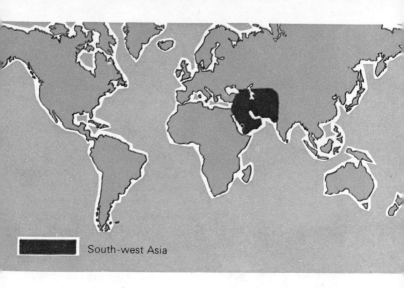

South-west Asia

South-west Asia

This region is being considered separately from the rest of Asia because it is the link area between Asia and Europe. It consists mostly of mountainous and desert terrain and it not only has an overlap of the two butterfly faunas, but also contains a great many species which are peculiar to this region. The area includes Arabia, Palestine, Mesopotamia, Turkey, Persia, Afghanistan and the neighbouring territories of Pakistan and Southern Russia.

It is in this region that special forms and rare species of *Parnassius*, *Colias* and Lycaenidae are to be found. The higher regions are rather inaccessible and probably new species will still be found there. To the east of the region the butterflies on the lower slopes are much the same as those found in India, but the population includes increasing numbers of European types towards the west through Syria into Turkey. Butterflies are sparse in the hotter, desert places but they are still present. Certain Pieridae, *Limnus chrysippus*, *Hypolimnas misippus* and even *Charaxes* are examples of species found in Saudi Arabia and South Yemen.

Limnas chrysippus

Precis orithya

Long-tailed Blue

Anthocharis eupheme

Limnas chrysippus is a persistent danaid which occurs from Africa right across to Australia. Many colour forms of this species exist. It can withstand hot, dry climate and is very hardy. It is closely related to the Monarch and the larva feeds on *Asclepias*. It is very common throughout south-west Asia. The wingspan is 5 to 8 cm (2 to 3 in).

Precis orithya is a common species of the Nymphalidae. It occurs in many geographical forms from Africa, right across Asia and beyond. It is a strong migrant, though not often seen in swarms. It is found at most times of the year, but in greatest numbers in autumn. An oasis insect, it is found by rivers, palm gardens, etc. The wingspan is 4 cm ($1\frac{1}{2}$ in).

The Long-tailed Blue *Lampides boeticus* is found from Europe right across Asia. This lycaenid butterfly migrates to Europe from its breeding grounds in south-west Asia. It is very common in gardens, open spaces and in grassland. The larvae feed on leguminous plants and are often found in gardens. It has a wingspan of about 2·5 cm (1 in).

Anthocharis eupheme is one of the orange tips of the family Pieridae and is found rather locally in stony desert and foothills of the less high mountains. It is not very common but occurs throughout Saudi Arabia, Iraq and Persia. The larvae feed on the leaves and pods of several Cruciferae. Its wingspan is around 5 cm (2 in).

Colias aurorina, a pierid, is not a very abundant species. It flies in June and July throughout higher ground in this region. One of the largest and most richly coloured of the genus *Colias,* it is much prized by collectors. The larvae feed on vetch and clover. Its wingspan is 5 cm (2 in).

Papilio alexanor belongs to the family Papilionidae. This swallowtail is found more in southern Europe but its range extends well into Persia. It is confined to higher mountains where it breeds above the tree line on various species of Umbelliferae. It has a wingspan of 5 to 8 cm (2 to 3 in).

Doritis apollinus is a pretty little papilionid which breeds in the north of this region and in the Balkans. It is not uncommon in Turkey but everywhere it keeps to high mountains, where it breeds on *Aristolochia.* It occurs once a year only, in June and July. The wingspan is 5 to 7 cm (2 to 2½ in).

Colias aurorina

Papilio alexanor

Doritis apollinus

BOOKS TO READ

The following useful books should be obtainable from bookshops and/or public libraries.

Australian Butterflies by I. F. B. Common. Jacaranda, Brisbane, 1964.
Butterflies (New Naturalist Series) by E. B. Ford. Collins, London.
A Butterfly Book for the Pocket by E. Sandars. Oxford University Press.
Complete British Butterflies in Colour by E. Mansell and L. H. Newman. Michael Joseph, London, 1968.
Concise Guide: Butterflies by J. Moucha. Hamlyn, London, 1968.
Create a Butterfly Garden by L. H. Newman. J. Baker, London.
A Field Guide to the Butterflies of Britain and Europe by L. H. Higgins and N. D. Riley. Collins, London, 1970.
The Observer's Book of Butterflies by W. J. Stokoe. Warne, London, 1964.
The Young Specialist Looks at Butterflies by G. Warnecke. Burke, London, 1964.

PLACES TO VISIT

IN BRITAIN

British Museum (Natural History), London. The Insect Gallery. By appointment it is possible to view the National Insect Collection, which is not open to the public.
Bristol Museum.
City of Liverpool Museum.
Drusilla's Cottage, Polegate, Sussex. Butterflies and moths from all parts of the world.
Exeter Museum

Worldwide Butterflies Ltd., Brighton and Lyme Regis. A wide selection of butterflies, equipment and books.
Worldwide Butterflies Ltd., Over Compton, Sherborne, Dorset. Butterfly farm.

IN AUSTRALIA

Australian National Insect Collection, Canberra.
University of Queensland.
National Museum, Melbourne.
Australian Museum, Sydney.

INDEX

Page numbers in bold type refer to illustrations.

Acleros mackenii 134, **135**
Acraea **45**, 126, 128
  A. anemosa 128, **128**
  A. egina 128, **128**
Acraeidae 44, 128
Adonis Blue **55**
Aeropetes tulbaghia 127
Ageronia velutina 118
  119
Aglais milberti 110, **110**
  A. urticae 37, 110
Agrias 47, 48, 63, 117, 118
  A. sardanapalus 118, **119**
Amathusiidae 52, **52**, 63, 138, 148
Amauris niavius 127, **127**
Ancyluris 53, 117
  A. formosissima **53**, **122**, 123
Angle-wings 108
Anthocharis cardamines 105
  A. eupheme 154, **154**
  A. sara 114, **114**
Apatura 46
  A. iris 65, 101
Aphnaeus hutchinsoni 131, **131**
Apollo Butterfly 59, 65, 106, **106**
Araschnia levana 31
Argynnis 16, 47, 65, 108
  A. diana 112, **112**
  A. paphia 101
  A. p. valezina 101
Arhopala centaurus 148, **149**

Bath whites 26, 27
Beaks 53
Birdwings, 6, 50, 59, 126, 142, 151
Black Hairstreak **14**, 15
Black papilios 117
Black Swallowtail 115, **115**
Blues 6, 32, 54-56, 63, 64, 65, 113
Boloria 108
  B. triclaris 112, **112**
Brassolidae 49, **49**, 121
Brimstone 7, 32, 57, 65, 66, 73, **104**, 105, 124
Browns 9, 16, 18, 41, 64, 65, 66, **100**

Brown Hairstreak **10**
Buckeye 110, **111**

Caligo 49, 117, 121
  C. atreus 121
Callicore 108, 120
  C. neglecta **120**, 121
Callitaera aurorina 118, **119**
Callithea sapphira **120**, **121**
Callophrys rubi 104
Camberwell Beauty see Mourning Cloak
Catagramma 47, 117, 120
  C. cynosura 118, **119**
  C. excelsior 118, **119**
Catopsilia 58, 108
  C. avellaneda 123, **125**
  C. philea 114
  C. scylla **150**, 151
Celastrina argiolus 102
Cethosia 48
  C. chrysippe 138, **138**
  C. myrina 148, **149**
Chalk Hill Blue 31, 102, **103**
Charaxes 48, 63, 126, 130, 138, 147, 153
  C. bohemani 130, **131**
  C. jasius saturnus 130, **131**
Chrysophanus virgaureae 103
Clouded Yellow **22**, 24, **32**, 57, 58, **58**, **81**, **104**, 105
Colias 66, 108, 153, 155
  C. aurorina 155, **155**
  C. caesonia 114
  C. crocea 57, 105
  C. eurydice 114
  C. hyale 57
Colorado Hairstreak **112**, 113
Colotis 31, 58, 63, 126
  C. erone 132, **132**
  C. euippe 132, **132**
Comma **6**, 10, 46, **46**, 98, 108, 110
Common Blue 102, **102**
Common Wood-nymph 109, **109**
Continental Large Copper 55
Coppers 6, 54-56, 65, 126
Crenis rosa 129, **129**
Cressida cressida **141**, 142
Crows 16, 28, 137
Cymothoe sangaris 129, **129**
Cyrestis 48, 147

C. thyodamas **146**, 147

Danaidea 9, 16, 28, 29, 42, **43**, 44, 46, 48, 109, 118, 127, 128, 133, 137, 145, 147, 154
Danaus 42
  D. melissa 137, **137**
  D. m. hamata 137
  D. plexippus 42, **43**, 109
Deione vanillae 111
Delias 58, 140
  D. aruna 140, **141**
  D. a. inferna 140
  D. harpalyce 140, **141**
  D. hyparete **150**, 151
  D. mysis 140, **141**
Dingy Skipper 107, **107**
Dismorphia 58, 108, 124
  D. orise 124, **125**
Dog Face Butterfly 114, **115**
Doleschallia bisaltidae 147, **149**
Doritis apollinus 155, **155**
Duke of Burgundy Fritillary 53, 102, **102**

Elymnias hypermnestra 145, **145**
Erebia 41, 65, 127
  E. aethiops 101
Eronia cleodora 132, **132**
Erycides zonara 124, **125**
Erycinidae 52, 53, **53**, 117, 123
Erynnis tages 107
Eudamus proteus 116
Euphydryas aurinia 101
Euploea 16, 32, 42
  E. callithae hansemanni 137, **137**
  E. diocletianus **146**, 147
  E. mulciber 145, **145**
Eurema 63, 108
  E. hecabe 148, **149**
  E. nicippe 113, **113**

Fiery Copper 103, **103**
Fritillaries 9, 16, 31, 46, 47, 64, 65, 66, 96, 102, 108, 111, 112

Giant Orange Tip 58
Giant Skipper 152
Glanville Fritillary 10, **35**

Gonepteryx menippe 124, **125**
Gonepteryx rhamni 105
Grass yellows 63, 148
Grayling **9**, 109
Great Purple Hairstreak 113, **113**
Green Hairstreak 104, **104**
Grizzled Skipper 26
Gulf Fritillary 111, **111**

Hairstreaks **6**, 10, 54-56, **56**, 64, 65, 113, 123, 131, 139, 148
Hamearis lucina 53, 102
Heath Fritillary 10
Hebomoia 58
    H. glaucippe **57**, 151
    H. vossi **150**, 151
Heliconiidae 44, **45**, 46, 118, 124
Heliconius 117, 118
    H. amaryllis **45**, 118, **119**
    H. dorus 118, **119**
Helicopis 123
    H. acis **122**, 123
Hesperiidae **6**, 61, **61**, 107, 116, 117, 124, 134, 152
Hestia 23, 42, 147
    H. leuconoe **146**, 147
Heteronympha 137
    H. merope 137, **137**
Holly Blue 31, 66, 102, **103**
Hypolimnas 48
    H. misippus 29, 128, 130, **130**, 153

Ialmenus evagoras 139, **139**
Ithomiidae 44, **44**, 118
Ituna phenarete 118, **119**
Ixias 58
    I. pyrene 148, 150

Jamides 148, **149**
Japanese Purple Emperor **7**

Kallima 48
    K. philarchus 148, **149**
Kaniska canace 147, **149**

Lacewing 48, 138, 148
Lampides boeticus 154
Large Blue 11, 56
Large Cabbage White 24
Large Copper 54
Large Skipper 10, **10**, **14**, **61**, 107, **107**

Large White 7, 23, 26, 31, 57
Leaf Butterfly 27, 48, **73**, 147-148
Lepidoptera 4, 23, 26, 27, 64
Leptidea 58
    L. sinapis 105
Libythea celtis celtoides **53**
Libythea geoffroyi 139, **139**
Libytheidae 52, **53**, 139
Limenitis 46, 147
    L. archippus 110
    L. camilla 65
Limnas alcippus 128, **128**
Limnas chrysippus 29, 128, 130, 153, 154, **154**
Liphyra brassolis major **139**, 140
Long-tailed Blue 154, **154**
Long-tailed Skipper 116, **116**
Lycaena 65, 83
    L. dispar 54
    L. phlaeas 54, 103
    L. sonorensis **112**, 113
Lycaenidae 6, 18, 32, 54, **55**, **56**, 66, 102, 103, 104, 113, 123, 126, 130, 131, 139, 140, 148, 153, 154
Lycorea 57, 118
    L. cleobaea 118, **119**
Lyropteryx apollonia **122**, 123
Lysandra corydon 102

Maculinea arion 11, 56
Map Butterfly 7, **7**, 10, 48, **48**, 147
Marbled White 26, 41, **41**
Marsh Fritillary 94, 95, **100**, 101
Meadow Brown **14**, 41
Mechanitis 57, 108, 118 124
Melampias trimenii 127
Melanargia galathea 41
Melanitis leda 41, 145, **145**
Melitaea 16, 47, 64, 108
    M. athalia 64
Milkweed 9, **9**, **14**, 24, **24**, 28, 42, 109, **109**, 110
Monarch *see* Milkweed
Morphidae 46, 50, 121-123
Morpho butterflies 49, 50, 52
Morpho 50, **51**, 117, 121-123, 148
    M. achilles 50, 121, **121**
    M. adonis 50
    M. aega 50, 121, **121**

M. aurora 50
M. catenarius 50
M. cypris 50
M. didius **122**, 123
M. eugenia 50
M. godarti 50
M. hecuba 50, **122**, 123
M. h. cisseis 50, 123
M. hercules 50
M. laertes 50
M. menelaus 50, **51**, 123
M. m. nestira 50
M. peleides 50
M. perseus 50
M. polyphemus 50
M. rhetenor 50, **122**, 123
M. r. pseudocypris 50, 123
M. sulkowski 50
M. theseus 50
Mourning Cloak 111, **111**
Myscelia orsis 118, **119**

Neocheritra amrita 148, **149**
Neophasia 57
Neptis 48, **146**, 147
Nessaea 120
    N. obrinus 120, **120**
Northern Brown **100**, 101
Nymphalidae 15, 18, 29, 37, 42, 46-48, **46-47**, **48**, 63, 65, 98, 101, 110, 111, 112, 118, 120, 121, 126, 127, 129, 130, 138, 147, 148, 154
Nymphalis antiopa 111
Nymphalis io 101

Ochlodes venata 107
Oenis gigas 109, **109**
Opsiphanes 49
Orange Tip 6, 7, 9, **14**, 15, 26, 57, 58, **72**, 73, **73**, 96, 105, **105**, 108, 154
Ornithoptera 50, 59, 60, 142
    O. alexandrae 142, **143**
    O. goliath 142, **143**
    O. paradisea **141**, 142
    O. priamus 142, **143**
    O. p. euphorion 142
    O. p. poseidon 142
Owl Butterfly 49, **49**, 117, **120**, 121

Painted Lady 23, 24, 25, 98, 138
Papilio 18, 59, 63, 108, 117, 126, 151
    P. ajax 116, **116**

P. alexanor 155, **155**
P. antheus 60
P. antimachus 60, 126,
133, **133**
P. asterias 115
P. bianor **59**
P. blumei **150**, 151
P. buddah 60
P. childrenae 124, **125**
P. coon 152, **152**
P. crino 60
P. dardanus 29, 127, 133,
135
P. demodocus 60, 134,
135
P. horishanus **150**, 151
P. leucaspis 60
P. machaon 31, 36, 58,
60, 106, 115
P. m. britannicus **36**
P. marcellus see P. ajax
P. nireus 60, 133, **135**
P. paris 60, **150**, 151
P. peranthus **150**, 151
P. podalirius 106
P. protesilaus 59, 124,
125
P. ridleyanus 128
P. sarpedon **150**, 151
P. serville 60
P. thoas 124, **125**
P. thyastes 60, 124, **125**
P. troilus 115
P. turnus 114
P. ulysses 60, **141**, 142
P. u. joesa 142
P weiskei 140, **141**
P. zalmoxis 60, 126, 133,
135
Papilionidae 6, 28, 42, 59,
59, 60, 62, 87, 93, 106,
114, 115, 116, 124,
133-134, 140, 142,
151-152, 155
Parantica sita **43**
Pararge aegeria 101
Pararge megera 137
Parnassius 108, 142, 153
P. apollo **25, 34**, 106
P. smintheus 115, **116**
Peacock 6, 7, 9, 28, 65, 72,
93, **100**, 101
Pereute 57
P. callinice 124, **125**
Perrhybris 57
P. lorena 124, **125**
Pierella dracontis 118, **119**
Pieridae 6, 18, 25, 31, 41,
42, 57-58, **57-58**, 62, 63,
93, 105, 113, 114, 123,
124, 126, 132, 140, 148,
151, 153, 164

Pieris 57
P. rapae 57
Polygonia 108
P. interrogationis 110
Polyommatus icarus 102
Polyura 48
P. delphis **146**, 147
P. pyrrhus 138, **138**
Precis 48, 63
P. coenia 110
P. genoveva 111
P. lavinia 111
P. octavia 31, 129, **129**
P. o. sesamus **129**
P. orithya 154, **154**
Prothoe calydonia **146**, 147
Purple Emperor 46, 65, **100**,
101
Purple Hairstreak 104, **104**

Question Mark 110, **110**

Red Admiral 6, 15, 24, 46,
65, 138
Red-barred Sulphur 114,
114
Rhopalocampta benjamini
152, **152**
Ringlet 41
Riodinidae 102

Salamis 130
S. parhassus 130, **131**
Sasakia charonda **7**
Satyridae 9, 16, 31, 41, **41**,
42, 46, 52, 63, 65, 66,
101, 108, 109, 118, 127,
137, 145
Satyrus alope 109
Scarce Swallowtail 106,
107
Silver-washed Fritillary 7,
97, 98, **100**, 101
Skippers 6, **7**, 16, 18, 23,
23, 32, 61, 63, 64, 65,
124
Small Copper 9, 10, 66, 94,
103, **103**
Small Heath 26
Small Tortoiseshell 7, **14**,
37, **37**, **38**, 110
Small White 57
Speckled Wood 66, **100**,
101
Spice-bush Swallowtail
115, **115**
Spindasis natalensis 130,
131
Stichopthalma camadeva

52, 148, **149**
Swallowtail 6, **6**, 7, 8, 10,
10, 15, **16-17**, 18, **18**, **23**,
28, 32, **32**, 36, **58**, 60, **60**,
80, 94, 106, **106**, 115,
124, 133, 142, 150, 155
Sword-tail 60, 124

Table Mountain Beauty 127,
127
Taenaris 52, 138
T. catops **52**, **138**, 139
Tailed skippers 116, 117
Thaumantis 52
T. diores 148, **149**
Thecla 56, 83
T. coronata 56, 123, **125**
T. crysalus 113
T. halesus 113
T. quercus 104
T. w-album 73
Thyridia confusa **44**
Thysonotis danis serapis
139, 140
Tiger Swallowtail 59, 114,
115
Tortoiseshell 9, 65, 66, 72
Tree Nymph 42
Trimen's Brown 127, **127**
Trogonoptera brookiana
152, **152**
Troides aeacus **150**, 151

Vanessa 46
V. gonerilla 138, **138**
V. g. ida 138
Vanessidi 6, 9, 16, 25, 37,
46, 47, 65, 66, 87, 96,
147
Viceroy 110, **110**

Wall Brown 137
Whites 6, 57, 65
White Admiral **9**, 31, **47**,
65
White Letter Hairstreak 73
Wood Nymph 41
Wood White 58, 105, **105**

Zerynthia 107
Z. polyxena 106–107,
107

SOME OTHER TITLES IN THIS SERIES

■ Arts
■ Domestic Animals and Pets
■ Domestic Science
■ Gardening

■ General Information
■ History and Mythology
■ Natural History
■ Popular Science

Arts
Antique Furniture/Architecture/Clocks and Watches/Glass for Collectors/Jewellery/Musical Instruments/Porcelain/Victoriana

Domestic Animals and Pets
Budgerigars/Cats/Dog Care/Dogs/Horses and Ponies/Pet Birds/Pets for Children/Tropical Freshwater Aquaria/Tropical Marine Aquaria

Domestic Science
Flower Arranging

Gardening
Chrysanthemums/Garden Flowers/Garden Shrubs/House Plants/ Plants for Small Gardens/Roses

General Information
Aircraft/Arms and Armour/Coins and Medals/Flags/ Freshwater Fishing/Guns/Military Uniforms/Motor Boats and Boating/National Costumes of the world/ Orders and Decorations/ Rockets and Missiles/ Sailing/Sailing Ships and Sailing Craft/Sea Fishing/Trains/Veteran and Vintage Cars/Warships

History and Mythology
Age of Shakespeare/Archaeology/Discovery of: Africa/ The American West/Australia/Japan/North America/South America/ Great Naval Battles/Myths and Legends of: Africa/Ancient Egypt/Ancient Greece/Ancient Rome/India/The South Seas/ Witchcraft and Black Magic

Natural History
The Animal Kingdom/Animals of Australia and New Zealand/ Animals of Southern Asia/Bird Behaviour/Birds of Prey/Butterflies/ Evolution of Life/Fishes of the world/ Fossil Man/A Guide to the Seashore/Life in the Sea/Mammals of the world/Monkeys and apes/Natural History Collecting/The Plant Kingdom/Prehistoric Animals/Seabirds/Seashells/Snakes of the world/Trees of the World/Tropical Birds/Wild Cats

Popular Science
Astronomy/Atomic Energy/Chemistry/Computers at Work/ The Earth/Electricity/Electronics/Exploring the Planets/Heredity The Human Body/Mathematics/Microscopes and Microscopic Life/ Undersea Exploration/The Weather Guide